Celebrating

THE KING JAMES VERSION

Text copyright © Rachel Boulding 2010
The author asserts the moral right
to be identified as the author of this work

Published by
The Bible Reading Fellowship
15 The Chambers, Vineyard
Abingdon OX14 3FE
United Kingdom
Tel: +44 (0)1865 319700

ISBN 978 1 84101 757 0

First published 2010

10 9 8 7 6 5 4 3 2 1 0

Acknowledgments

Extracts from the Authorised Version of the Bible (The King James Bible), the rights in which are vested in the Crown, are reproduced by permission of the Crown's Patentee, Cambridge University Press.

New English Bible copyright © 1961, 1970 by Oxford university Press and Cambridge University Press.

Scripture quotations from The New Revised Standard Version of the Bible, Anglicised Edition, copyright © 1989, 1995 by the Division of Christian Education of the National Council of the Churches of Christ in the United States of America, are used by permission. All rights reserved.

Scripture quotations taken from the Holy Bible, New International Version, copyright © 1973, 1978, 1984, 1995 by International Bible Society. Used by permission of Hodder & Stoughton Publishers, a member of the Hachette Livre UK Group. All rights reserved. 'NIV' is a registered trademark of International Bible Society. UK trademark number 1448790.

Scriptures quoted from the Good News Bible published by The Bible Societies/HarperCollins Publishers Ltd, UK © American Bible Society 1966, 1971, 1976, 1992, used with permission.

Extracts from The Book of Common Prayer of 1662, the rights of which are vested in the Crown in perpetuity within the United Kingdom, are reproduced by permission of Cambridge University Press, Her Majesty's Printers.

Copyright material is included from *Common Worship: Services and Prayers for the Church of England*; copyright © The Archbishops' Council 2000, and material from it is reproduced with permission.

The lines from *Ash Wednesday*, *Murder in the Cathedral*, and *Four Quartets* are taken from *The Complete Poems and Plays of T.S. Eliot* (Faber, 1962). Used by permission.

A catalogue record for this book is available from the British Library

Printed in India by Thomson Press India Ltd

Celebrating

THE KING JAMES VERSION

DEVOTIONAL READINGS
FROM THE CLASSIC TRANSLATION

Rachel Boulding

To the memory of Archibald Harold Garratt
(7 July 1899–14 August 1986), much-loved grandfather,
and to Martin James Brooke, beloved husband

Acknowledgments

Particular thanks are due to my mother, Joyce Boulding, who read the earliest versions of these readings and supplied invaluable comments. She provided much-needed common sense, theological *nous* and profound spirituality born of a lifetime of prayer and faith.

I would also like to thank Naomi Starkey of BRF for suggesting this book and helping enormously to shape it. I couldn't have done it without her.

Finally I want to acknowledge my huge gratitude to my son, Thomas, and my husband, Martin, who put up with me during the writing, and managed to find some football to watch to help pass the time while waiting for me to finish.

This book is dedicated to Martin and to my grandfather, who inspired it all.

Contents

Foreword

The Authorised Version can make a better claim than any other book to have shaped and enriched one of the world's great languages. During the last 400 years, many of its phrases—'turning the other cheek', 'the root of the matter' and 'prodigal son', to name but three—have become part of our linguistic arsenal.

But there is more, for there are few texts that have so encouraged and nurtured the potential of the English language to achieve beauty and clarity. Most significantly, of course, it is this translation of the Bible that, for centuries, has nourished our public worship and personal spirituality.

I chair the 2011 Trust (www.2011trust.org), which, since its launch in 2007, has worked to prepare a range of celebrations to mark the impact of this great book on English-speaking peoples around the world.

It is a real pleasure, therefore, to be able to write a foreword to this new publication. Appropriately, *Celebrating the King James Version* brings to us all the opportunity to recapture some of the riches of language and the deep messages of this Bible. Rachel Boulding has brought together a treasury of spiritual insights, hewn from the quarry of her own experience, friendships and reading. Her clarity of language and the definition of her imagery aptly resonate with the qualities of the translation itself.

I am also conscious, as a politician, of the political motivations of King James I when he commissioned the Authorised Version. It was a sincere attempt to bring unity to a very divided kingdom as diverging factions within the churches threatened to pull the kingdom apart. It is gratifying, then, that Rachel embraces the world of politics as well as those of work, leisure and family, to bring home to us the applications of the Bible to our lives.

The Authorised Version adorns our language; this book of thoughtful insights and prompts to prayer adorns that text. I commend its use as a simple but profound way to commemorate this year with gratitude to God and with thankfulness for the Bible in our language. I sincerely hope that it will encourage you to become involved in the many other ways in which the 2011 Trust is proclaiming the importance of this year and this translation.

Frank Field MP
Chairman of the 2011 Trust

Why the King James Version is so special

The King James Version of the Bible is one of the first books I can remember reading. As a small child, I was struck by the strange, old-fashioned dark type, the odd words and expressions—'thee' and 'thou', 'seeketh', 'sojourn' and 'tabernacle'. I didn't have much clue about what it all meant, but I did grasp something: it was important and it had the unmistakable stamp of authority.

Of course, this is because these are the words of Scripture. We don't approach the Bible like any other book that might contain history, poetry, biography, law and other types of writing. This is Holy Writ, and we come reverently, looking for the words of eternal life—words on which we can base our whole existence. These words set our spines tingling. Like the disciples on the road to Emmaus, our hearts 'burn within us' as we read or hear them (Luke 24:32).

But with the KJV there is something else, too. Because the translation was done in a particular way, at a particular time in the development of the English language and English literature, its words and phrasing are especially rich (Dr Alison Shell talks about this in a straightforward and illuminating way in her afterword). Like good poetry, the chosen words suggest depths and layers of meaning, neatly and movingly. They also have echoes of Shakespeare, having been produced at about the same time (although this translation came too late for the playwright himself; he used the Geneva Bible of 1560).

The language of the KJV has a special vividness, which comes partly from its origins in this historical period, when the language was changing rapidly. But it was made to sound deliberately old-fashioned, harking back to earlier English translations, 80 years before it was put together in the years leading up to publication in 1611. In fact, it draws very heavily on William Tyndale's translation of the 1520s and '30s. A computer analysis in 1998 suggested that 83 per cent of the KJV New Testament and 76 per cent of its Old Testament came from Tyndale.

The idea that it wasn't meant to sound like everyday language (like what we used to call 'Gas Board English') is reflected in what John Donne, the poet and Dean of St Paul's, spoke of in one of his sermons, preached a few years after 1611. He referred to the style of the Bible in its original tongues as having 'a delicacy, and harmony, and melody of language... and not with barbarous, or triviall, or homely language'. He refers slightingly to 'Translations, which could not maintaine the Majesty, nor preserve the elegancies of the Originall' (from Sermon LV 'Preached on the Penitentiall Psalms').

The KJV might not sound chatty, but it uses sharp phrases that immediately give an echo to so much of our experience. Hence, 'Lord, I believe; help thou mine unbelief,' says the father of a boy with a spirit (Mark 9:24). 'Unbelief' is a fairly literal version of the Greek *apistia*, and has a raw directness. It conjures up so much more than the more awkward 'I do believe; help me overcome my unbelief' (NIV).

The KJV also first coined many words and expressions that have become part of the language—so much so that most people don't necessarily think of them as biblical, and usually attribute them to Shakespeare. So we have 'escaped with the skin of my teeth' (Job 19:20), 'they shall reap the whirlwind' (Hosea 8:7), 'the signs of the times' (Matthew 16:3), 'a law unto themselves' (Romans 2:14), 'the powers that be' (Romans 13:1) and many more. It's not surprising that it is still the best-selling book in the world, despite the huge growth in modern versions.

How to use this book

Most of this book was written originally as daily readings for the BRF *New Daylight* notes, using the KJV and other versions, too. They were and are designed to equip and encourage Christians in their faith each day, and not to offer literary or academic commentary on the words of the KJV translation. The short sections attempt to draw out some devotional aspects of each passage, as they relate to the lives of believers as they seek God.

I was always looking to answer the question, 'What do these words say to us now in our life of faith?' So, while I might sometimes refer, for example, to a word in Greek (I'm afraid I don't know much Hebrew), this is not so much to explain each element in the text as to use it as part of a wider reflection on what it might mean for our spirituality and discipleship now. Readers searching for an analysis of the qualities of the KJV's language as a literary exercise, or a scholarly examination of every aspect of a passage, should look elsewhere.

In shaping the material for this book, I have tried to draw out some elements of the KJV's language and to explain the words that have now become harder to understand. But I have been surprised at how little I have needed to 'translate' the KJV into modern English. Often, it is crystal clear. Sometimes, too, there are just one or two words that, once explained, make a whole passage easily comprehensible.

When writing, I was limited to a few verses and a tight word count for my notes on them. This is why some of the passages are marked 'abridged' where I have left out parts of verses: this is entirely because of space constraints. It has also meant that I have had to pick up on just one or two ideas about any particular passage. Obviously there is much, much more that could be said about all of them.

The sections of passages are arranged in the order they appear in the Bible, with two themed parts at the end (focusing on St Richard of Chichester and Julian of Norwich). There are also some seasonal sections, such as those for Christmas and Holy Week. This means that the sections can be read in any order. It's probably better not to start at the beginning, but to dip in and start with whatever section appeals or seems appropriate. Within each section, though, the passages do usually flow on from the first to the last. They can be read one per day, as part of a time of reflection and prayer, perhaps at the same time in the morning or evening each day, or in groups of several during a longer quiet time.

Psalms 21—41

Beneath the immediate emotional impact of the psalms, there is a great deal going on. In one way, they seem straightforward—they are cries of pain or delight from one individual, direct to us. Their talk of sleepless nights or plotting enemies, as well as their thankfulness for blessings received, are specific enough to prompt our memories and imagination, but vague enough not to tie things down too much. This last quality, though, and the fact that we know so little about when they were composed, keeps the psalms for ever mysterious. All this, of course, is why they retain their power after thousands of years and we still use them in worship, prayer and study today. They tell us about how down-to-earth humans relate to their creator.

The whole book of 150 psalms encompasses inspiring poetry as well as terrifying curses—the raw guts of human emotion. The part that I will be considering here, Psalms 21—41, is usually classified as the second half of Book I (out of five books). Here, there are psalms about God's covenant with his people and praise, but laments, too. There's no polite disengagement from feeling and no apathy, either—they have real bite.

The King James Version brings out the poetic quality of the original but is still clear and direct, while suggesting the heartfelt emotional depths to which it refers. So in Psalm 22:10, 'thou art my God from my mother's belly' says more to me than the NRSV's 'since my mother bore me you have been my God', and Psalm 29:2 in the KJV, 'worship the Lord in the beauty of holiness', seems more evocative than 'worship the Lord in holy splendour' (NRSV).

Many psalms that we might think are from the KJV, though, are actually taken from the version in the Book of Common Prayer (BCP), which uses the older translation by Miles Coverdale, first published in 1535. When the BCP was revised in 1662 from its earlier editions a century before, the compilers didn't bring in the more recent translation that had been done in the meantime, in 1611, but kept the old one from the 1500s. Perhaps they didn't see much need for change. This, and the use of many other metrical and hymn versions of the psalms, does mean, however, that we don't know the KJV Psalter so well from using it in worship.

While most scholars don't back the traditional idea that the psalms were written by King David, there are few definite details to put in place of it. We don't even know for certain when they were written, though there are various speculations about some psalms being older than others. There is a sense, though, in which it doesn't matter what originally prompted each psalm. While it is helpful to know the background, what concerns us here is what they are saying to us now and how they can bring us nearer to God. As I hope we'll see, they have a real potency to inspire our yearning for him.

Why does God seem to hide?

My God, my God, why hast thou forsaken me? Why art thou so far from helping me, and from the words of my roaring? O my God, I cry in the daytime, but thou hearest not; and in the night season, and am not silent. But thou art holy, O thou that inhabitest the praises of Israel. Our fathers trusted in thee: they trusted, and thou didst deliver them.

The power of the raw emotion here—familiar from Holy Week readings—hits us immediately, even before we remember Jesus using these words on the cross (Matthew 27:46; Mark 15:34). Yet this is a sacred text about how human beings relate to the Creator. In the Gospel writers' view, these holy words—however unholy they might seem—had seeped into Jesus' soul, to the extent that he could make them his own in the extremes of his physical pain. Quite apart from anything else, this is a model of how to incorporate the insights of scripture into our lives.

We might struggle to admit it but most of us, however spiritual we are, have felt abandoned by God at some time. Why does God seem to hide away? There are partial answers, such as the basic human urge always to be looking for more. Even if we had a cast-iron solution, though, would it make us happier? Those times of feeling dumped by God are one of the mysterious facts of life; but we needn't just use that as an excuse to let ourselves off from searching for God. There are things we can do. We can strive be honest and admit that we do feel distant from God. This should also help us to be sympathetic when we face the spiritual difficulties of others.

The agony of seeming far from God can also increase our yearning for him, making us more determined to persevere in prayer, worship, talking about faith, reading the Bible and other study. It's not so much a matter of will as of gently reminding ourselves that God is here, as he has been in our past, whether we feel his presence now or not.

REFLECTION

'I believe in the sun, even when it doesn't shine. I believe in love, even when I don't feel it. I believe in God, even when he is silent.'
Written by a German Jew suffering Nazi persecution

The balance of pain and praise

But thou art he that took me out of the womb: thou didst make me hope when I was upon my mother's breasts. I was cast upon thee from the womb: thou art my God from my mother's belly. Be not far from me; for trouble is near; for there is none to help… I will declare thy name unto my brethren: in the midst of the congregation will I praise thee. Ye that fear the Lord, praise him; all ye the seed of Jacob, glorify him; and fear him, all ye the seed of Israel.

In the previous reading, straight after the agony ('I cry…') came 'But thou art holy…'. Even in the middle of depicting his pain, the psalmist has to admit that God is a loving Creator. Throughout the first part of this long psalm, complaints alternate with praise, until there is a turning point (v. 22) and the poem continues to its end in hope and thankfulness.

This is a pattern in a number of psalms: extremes of grief are followed swiftly by assurance and thanksgiving. Some scholars put this sudden mood swing down to the way the psalms might be sung in worship, perhaps using different singers for the different parts, and having some sense of question and answer. Others think that the more confident parts might come from a different poem that has been spliced into the words of lament.

However we interpret these varied moods, they have now been brought together in a single psalm, where they reflect different parts of a whole. It is as if you can't have one without the other; neither alone gives the full picture. Sharp complaint isn't complete on its own, and, while giving praise to God is a vital part of our daily lives, we shouldn't make it our only note, as we shouldn't ignore the suffering around us and within us.

This is one sense in which the psalter is sometimes described as the Old Testament in miniature. It encompasses both the extremes of pain and the daily thankfulness of our life with and in God.

REFLECTION

Take a moment to remember a turning point in your life, when you suddenly found hope. Perhaps the change became clear only with hindsight. Was there a realisation of some truth about love that tipped the balance?

Fear no ill

The Lord is my shepherd; I shall not want. He maketh me to lie down in green pastures: he leadeth me beside the still waters... Yea, though I walk through the valley of the shadow of death, I will fear no evil: for thou art with me; thy rod and thy staff they comfort me.

Most of us have vivid memories connected with this, the best-loved psalm in the whole book. Many can recall singing it at school and, of course, it is often used at funerals. The KJV brings out the poetry of this anthem of hope, in a way that enables it to stay with us in times of desolation.

Strangely, Psalm 23 stands out from the rest of the psalter in its message of reassurance. Most psalms are not comforting like this—they have other things to say. Sometimes, however, this word of hope is just what we need. We shouldn't be ashamed or afraid of welcoming it. The Christian life isn't all a matter of bracing activity, certainty, dogged faithfulness or even exultant praise. Sometimes, we need to acknowledge our needs humbly before God and let the reality of his care flood through our senses.

Of course, there are times when we do need to be made to lie down in green pastures, times when we need to realise that our rushing around won't solve all our problems. As T.S. Eliot writes in *Ash Wednesday* (1930), 'Teach us to care and not to care / Teach us to sit still.'

As we saw in Psalm 22, we can feel distant from God, but, equally, we can be our own worst enemy and run away from him by ourselves. What are we afraid of when we wriggle away from the love that he offers? God wants to fill our cups to overflowing with his abundant life. Try reading the psalm again, and work out the areas of your life where you need to let God's grace flow in.

REFLECTION

Do you have a memory of reassurance associated with Psalm 23? If you do, take the chance to give thanks for it now. Even if you don't, thank God for the ways in which the people you love and have loved are cared for by God.

Carry on searching

The Lord is my light and my salvation; whom shall I fear? The Lord is the strength of my life; of whom shall I be afraid? When the wicked, even mine enemies and my foes, came upon me to eat up my flesh, they stumbled and fell... therefore will I offer in his tabernacle sacrifices of joy; I will sing, yea, I will sing praises unto the Lord... When thou saidst, Seek ye my face; my heart said unto thee, Thy face, Lord, will I seek. Hide not thy face far from me... I had fainted, unless I had believed to see the goodness of the Lord in the land of the living.

This is an inspiring and thought-provoking psalm, which will be known to some in the jaunty musical setting by Handel, which is one of the Chandos Anthems (pieces first written for the private chapel of the Duke of Chandos). It is the only time in the Old Testament when God is described as 'my light' (though in Isaiah 10:17 and 60:19–20 he is seen as the light of Israel and 'thine everlasting light').

Yet, even here, there isn't just a bland jollity. As we saw with Psalm 23, where God's comfort was felt against a background of loneliness and death, so here God's light brightens the psalmist's path in the face of his enemies. As the American scholar Walter Brueggemann comments, 'The confidence of verses 1–6 of course does not eliminate trouble from life, and this deep faith does not cause the speaker to deny reality or to remain mute about it. But verses 1–6 surely provide a trustful, buoyant context in which trouble is handled and understood differently' (*The Message of the Psalms*, Augsburg, 1984).

The psalm seems to be something of a reply to the questions of psalms such as Psalm 22. One of the issues that psalm seemed to be grappling with was how we cope when God appears to be far away. This psalm suggests that we can keep going through the fearful, tough times using our worship, prayer and praise (vv. 6–8). We need to keep making the effort to seek God's face (vv. 8–9). We have to carry on searching, even when it seems we're getting nowhere.

--- **REFLECTION** ---

In what simple ways can I seek God's face today? Perhaps think over the possibilities offered by prayer, listening, action, reading and seeing him in others.

The beauty of holiness

Give unto the Lord, O ye mighty, give unto the Lord glory and strength. Give unto the Lord the glory due unto his name; worship the Lord in the beauty of holiness... The voice of the Lord is powerful; the voice of the Lord is full of majesty... The Lord sitteth upon the flood; yea, the Lord sitteth King for ever. The Lord will give strength unto his people; the Lord will bless his people with peace.

After all the soul-searching of the earlier psalms, here is a hymn of praise to God. It resounds with God's voice as he thunders on the primeval waters, the 'flood'. If we want to seek God's face—as we were doing in the previous reading—we can do this wherever we are, as we can always look at his creation in the world around us.

This psalm might have been sung at the autumn festival in the temple in Jerusalem. Many scholars think it is one of the oldest parts of the psalter and that it reuses pagan forms of praise, such as a hymn to Baal, the storm god. This shouldn't worry us: after all, many of our festivals, especially Christmas, involve Christianised versions of pre-Christian strivings towards God.

Even if our built environment is soul-destroying and the sky is dark, we can always reflect God's creativity by making our worship and individual prayer beautiful. The phrase 'the beauty of holiness' (v. 2) can sometimes be hijacked by those who enjoy fussy worship. Others, however—embarrassed by the excesses of past obsessions with ceremony—throw out the baby with the bathwater and make worship ugly instead. There is no need to veer to extremes. The beauty of holiness can be carefully crafted (elaborate, even) but it needn't always be. It needs a sincere heart, inspired by the beauty of God's creation and truth, and this can be seen in carefully orchestrated ceremonial just as much as pared-down plainness.

In the movement from the glory of verse 10, as God is enthroned, to the blessing of peace (v. 11), Walter Brueggemann sees a link with the angels' song at the first Christmas: 'Glory to God in the highest, and on earth peace, good will toward men' (Luke 2:14). The cosmic king brings a new well-being to the world. So the raw power is put to a purpose. This is not just a show of strength but also a more benevolent ordering of the world so that all can flourish under God's protection.

--- REFLECTION ---

How can you foster today the beauty of holiness that honours God and encourages peace?

Mourning turned into dancing

I will extol thee, O Lord; for thou hast lifted me up, and hast not made my foes to rejoice over me... For his anger endureth but a moment; in his favour is life: weeping may endure for a night, but joy cometh in the morning. And in my prosperity I said, I shall never be moved... thou didst hide thy face, and I was troubled. I cried to thee, O Lord... Thou hast turned for me my mourning into dancing: thou hast put off my sackcloth, and girded me with gladness; to the end that my glory may sing praise to thee, and not be silent. O Lord my God, I will give thanks unto thee for ever.

This is a thanksgiving to God, moving from praise to trouble and fear of death, and then out the other side to thanks for deliverance. It contains words that have provided comfort to many over the centuries: 'weeping may endure for a night, but joy cometh in the morning' (v. 5).

It is more than a simple movement from darkness to light, however, as the troubles described here are at least partly of the author's own making. It was in prosperity that he felt secure: he didn't need God (v. 6). He is rather like the rich man in Luke 12:16–21, who planned bigger barns for his goods and took his ease. He laid up treasure for himself but was not rich towards God. Then his soul was required that night. Some of this seems horribly familiar to those of us with mortgages and too much clutter.

The psalm as a whole, in its 12 verses, reveals that the psalmist felt favoured by God, but this was an illusion. When life became tough, perhaps through ill health, and he couldn't sense God's presence, he realised that his existence was like death. Thankfully, he had the sense to do something about it and call out to God. It makes me wonder in which areas of my life I am building up a self-sufficiency, as if I have all the answers on my own. How can I let God into those parts that I like to hug to myself? This can spread to material wealth, as well as self-giving in hospitality and kindness to others. Perhaps I need reminding of what we say at the offertory in church: 'All things come from you, and of your own do we give you.'

REFLECTION

'For whom is your money good news?'
From a sermon by Archbishop Rowan Williams

The ups and downs of faith

In thee, O Lord, do I put my trust; let me never be ashamed: deliver me in thy righteousness. Bow down thine ear to me; deliver me speedily... Into thine hand I commit my spirit: thou hast redeemed me, O Lord God of truth... I will be glad and rejoice in thy mercy: for thou hast considered my trouble; thou hast known my soul in adversities.

This psalm dramatises what it feels like to live by faith in God. It alternates between stirring expressions of hope and trust, and hints at various kinds of anxiety and suffering. Some readers have suggested that these feel like different poems, while others (with whom I agree) point to these differences as being different moods within the same person.

This is such a telling picture of the life of faith because it highlights the ups and downs of our covenant relationship with God. In the end, the psalmist knows that he can trust God's mercy because God knows him and what he is going through (v. 7). This is like the wonderfully comforting opening of Psalm 139: 'Thou hast searched me and known me...'. God is with us in our pain, even before we remember Jesus entering into our humanity.

The psalm as a whole seems to reflect crucial aspects of our Christian lives because of how it encompasses assurance about God's love and ultimate victory with a genuine sense of how bad life can be in the meantime. ('Deliver me speedily' in verse 2 has a ring of desperation, and the seemingly modern word 'speedily' isn't in the Book of Common Prayer version, which says just 'make haste to deliver me'. It's another moment when the KJV surprises us by the powerful directness of its language.) So verse 5 has 'Into thine hand I commit my spirit'—which are the last words of Jesus on the cross (Luke 23:46) and what might seem like the lowest point. Yet they are followed immediately by 'thou hast redeemed me'—setting the pain in a wider context again. We may be at one with God's victory but it doesn't always feel like that in the daily grind. We are still mired in sin and we still have to deal with its consequences.

In this 'already but not yet' situation, our faith needs all the more to be centred on the God who is with us through it all.

--- REFLECTION ---

'Search me, O God, and know my heart: try me, and know my thoughts: and see if there be any wicked way in me, and lead me in the way everlasting'
(Psalm 139:23–24).

O make but trial of his love

This poor man cried, and the Lord heard him... O taste and see that
the Lord is good: blessed is the man that trusteth in him... Keep
thy tongue from evil, and thy lips from speaking guile... The Lord is
nigh unto them that are of a broken heart; and saveth such as be of a
contrite spirit. Many are the afflictions of the righteous: but the Lord
delivereth him out of them all.

This is the first of the psalms we have looked at that has a strong sense
of God's concern for the poor. Of course, this means those with few
possessions or resources, but it can also include those who are destitute
in terms of their spirit. So it can bring together our proper concern for
the poor—particularly those in developing countries—and for our friends
nearer home and ourselves, who are so often poverty-stricken in terms of
faith.

There's also a stronger sense of community here than in the other
psalms we've looked at. This alternates throughout the psalm with an
individual's account of being saved from trouble by the Lord. It also has an
element of teaching, making it similar to the book of Proverbs and other
Wisdom literature in the Old Testament. There is a wonderful feeling of
finding blessings in private experience and sharing them with others: 'O
taste and see...'. This is intensified if we recall the Tate and Brady hymn
version of this psalm, 'Through all the changing scenes of life': 'O magnify
the Lord with me / With me exalt his name / When in distress to him I
called / He to my rescue came.'

Part of the gospel we have to proclaim is that Christians are not life-
denying miseries. I remember the evangelist Canon Michael Green quoting
'O taste and see...' to a group of students, while taking a sip of the college
port; it was the type of message we could relate to.

As so often with the psalms, there is a healthy balance. As well as the
good things in and for life, there is a genuine appreciation of the reality of
suffering (vv. 18–19). But, as always in the psalms, there is something we
can do, however small it may seem: 'Keep thy tongue from evil' (v. 13).

--- REFLECTION ---

*In your worship, in what ways can you taste, see and savour the Lord's
goodness? Is there anything you might do to share this joy with others?*

Praise God in the middle of grief

Plead my cause, O Lord, with them that strive with me: fight against them that fight against me... Let their way be dark and slippery: and let the angel of the Lord persecute them. For without cause have they hid for me their net in a pit, which without cause they have digged for my soul... Let them shout for joy, and be glad, that favour my righteous cause... And my tongue shall speak of thy righteousness and of thy praise all the day long.

The atmosphere here is dark and full of anxiety. The speaker has been let down by those he trusted. He appeals to God in bold terms for help, demanding judgment on those who have hurt him, as well as judgment on himself—for he has nothing to fear from God; he knows that he will be vindicated.

In this psalm, the speaker isn't asking for quite the extremes of bloody revenge against his enemies that occur in other parts of the psalms, such as Psalm 137:9, where the speaker calls for the deaths of his enemies' children. He is in that place where he knows he has been treated unfairly and cries out for justice—as I hope most people would.

This isn't a comfortable place to be, poised as it is between an ugly desire for revenge and a smug self-pity that can't see past our own hurt and innocence. When I experienced something like this—in a workplace where it seemed to us that the senior management was treating the juniors as less than human, cogs to be manipulated at will—some of us started a prayer group to try to focus our anger. We didn't want it to turn inwards into sourness but instead offered it to God. We also tried to talk to the management, so that our prayers didn't dwindle into over-spiritualised introspection or martyrdom complexes.

It was important to realise that our sufferings were hardly cosmic: no one died. Better to see God's concern for justice and try to avoid the self-dramatising paranoia to which this psalm veers dangerously close. We thought it was vital, too, to look for God in the midst of a bad situation, just as the psalmist manages to praise God, even though his suffering is far from over (vv. 27–28).

PRAYER

God our Father, help us to seek your justice in every situation and praise you in the midst of our troubles.

Learning love and generosity

Fret not thyself because of evildoers, neither be thou envious against
the workers of iniquity. For they shall soon be cut down like the grass,
and wither as the green herb. Trust in the Lord, and do good; so shalt
thou dwell in the land, and verily thou shalt be fed... Commit thy
way unto the Lord; trust also in him; and he shall bring it to pass...
For evildoers shall be cut off: but those that wait upon the Lord, they
shall inherit the earth.

This psalm begins with a crucial dilemma in the life of faith: what do we
do about sinful people? We can follow the Lord with all the goodness
that he gives us, but, sooner or later, we'll come crashing up against the fact
that some people turn away from him.

This opening verse suggests an approach like Jesus' when he speaks of
the mote and the beam (Matthew 7:3–4). We should attend to our own
faults first—which should keep us busy enough—before correcting others.
The verses that follow suggest we can also 'trust... and do good... Commit
thy way' (vv. 3, 5).

The psalm assures us that, if we wait patiently for God, 'evildoers shall
be cut off' (v. 9). This goes against the grain of our worldly wisdom. If I'm
truthful, I'm jealous that the evildoers get away with it. It's not always
much comfort to think that they will be judged eventually. It seems too
late. Perhaps I'd secretly like to do evil and prosper myself, instead of all
this dull striving after good. That's looking at it from a skewed perspective,
however—the life of faith isn't really about trying desperately to be a goody-
two-shoes, as if God wants us for the strength of our will. No, it's all about
love. God loved us while we were still sinners (Romans 5:8) and we can
respond to his love. We can all join with those in heaven, rejoicing over the
one who strayed and was found (Luke 15:4–7). If we truly love, we'll be
generous and be glad to have more people at the heavenly party to rejoice
in God's love, rather than going around nit-picking.

--- **REFLECTION** ---

*Think about some of holiest people you have met. Does their approach to life
make you want to pick over the scabs of others' faults?*

— PSALM 38:1–2, 5, 21–22 —

The way out of filthy folly

O Lord, rebuke me not in thy wrath: neither chasten me in thy hot displeasure. For thine arrows stick fast in me, and thy hand presseth me sore... My wounds stink and are corrupt because of my foolishness... Forsake me not, O Lord: O my God, be not far from me. Make haste to help me, O Lord my salvation.

There is a version of this psalm translated by Sir Philip Sidney in the 16th century. It uses some of the same words as the KJV ('My wounds putrify and stink'). The psalmist's complaints fit well in the vivid introspective poetry of Elizabethan England. The type of individual reflection and shifting perspective that we find in Hebrew poetry is matched by the mood of English poets centuries later. Of course, the Elizabethan and later 17th-century poets (such as John Donne and George Herbert) were steeped in the psalms and influenced by their approach.

This, one of the seven penitential psalms traditionally used by the Church in devotions surrounding the confession of sins, suggests how we can all find our own version of the psalmists' struggles. Some people find great benefit in writing spiritual journals, diaries or poems. It might be worth trying, even if you haven't thought of yourself as any good at expressing your thoughts in this way.

The psalmist is unsparing in his honesty. Unfashionable as it may seem now, there are times when we need this searing vision of ourselves. Life isn't all a warm bath. However much we try to insulate ourselves, we know really that being a Christian doesn't and shouldn't take us out of the suffering of the world. Sometimes we need a kick-start.

The psalmist is able to see where he stands and do something about it by turning to God. This can make it sound so simple. What is our problem, that we find it so difficult? That's where the poetry, of both the original Hebrew and of this translation, comes in. It makes vivid the questions about our sin and God's salvation. It reminds me of another telling combination of music and poetry (see below), which conveys a vital message with devastating simplicity.

--- **REFLECTION** ---

O what peace we often forfeit,
O what needless pain we bear,
All because we do not carry
Everything to God in prayer!

Joseph Scriven (1855)

Beyond being nice

When thou with rebukes dost correct man for iniquity, thou makest his beauty to consume away like a moth: surely every man is vanity. Hear my prayer, O Lord, and give ear unto my cry; hold not thy peace at my tears: for I am a stranger with thee, and a sojourner, as all my fathers were. O spare me, that I may recover strength, before I go hence, and be no more.

———————————

As we saw with Psalm 38, the KJV helps to bring out the force of the personal lament—the stark sense of words clothed in tears and having only God to turn to. Again, it seems like a simple choice, but one that we clearly find anything but straightforward.

At the beginning of the psalm, the speaker tries to keep a check on himself, so that he doesn't fall into sinful speech: 'I said, I will take heed to my ways, that I sin not with my tongue' (v. 1). This does not reduce his suffering, however: if anything, it makes it worse. Then, in contrast to those who build up earthly treasures, he realises that humankind is merely vanity (or 'a puff of wind', as the NEB has it) and matters little in the cosmic scheme of things.

It is as if he has realised, as some people never do, that human effort is never going to be enough. The religion of being a 'decent chap' doesn't actually work. Just recall a few generalised, inoffensive, non-faith-based school assemblies or motivational talks about being nice, and you'll know what I mean about this hollowness. Our psalmist knows better and turns to God. Crucially, he also includes recognition of his sins.

Turning to God isn't simply a passive act, like waiting to be rescued. Rather, it involves the work of seeing what we have done to harm ourselves and others. That done, though, the rewards can come quickly—sometimes in a sense of God's presence with us now, sometimes just the knowledge that, while we might not be able to feel anything special, we are at least aiming for the right path. This transforms the situation from one of anger, frustration and loneliness to one of hope, love and comfort.

——————— **REFLECTION** ———————

In what areas am I trying to be a nice person on my own and without God?

The tide can turn

I waited patiently for the Lord; and he inclined unto me, and heard my cry. He brought me up also out of an horrible pit, out of the miry clay, and set my feet upon a rock, and established my goings. And he hath put a new song in my mouth, even praise unto our God: many shall see it, and fear, and shall trust in the Lord... I delight to do thy will, O my God: yea, thy law is within my heart... Withhold not thou thy tender mercies from me, O Lord: let thy lovingkindness and thy truth continually preserve me.

Here is a song of hope and thankfulness for God's mercies, followed by a lament. Usually in the psalms, the order is the other way round: grief is followed by praise of the Lord, who has saved the speaker, even if all the pain isn't over yet. Here, however, the hope is first. Walter Brueggemann describes 'I waited patiently' (v. 1) as 'a weak rendering... which might better be translated "I hope intensely for Yahweh." Indeed, all other hopes were exhausted... The hope was against all the evidence in the conviction that Yahweh could work a genuine newness. The hope was not disappointed.'

This is the kind of conviction that perhaps we hardly ever allow ourselves to risk, but which can be vindicated. Sometimes the international situation looks bleak, but the tide can turn, as it has done in various situations throughout history, such as in South Africa at the end of the apartheid era.

The change of mood at verse 11 is abrupt, but there are enough links between the two halves to seal them together. This anguished lament is why the Church has traditionally used this psalm at Good Friday services. We can find here the sufferings of Jesus, joined with those of countless others.

The unusual way in which the psalm ends—with the speaker still beset by trouble after being helped, but appealing to God—has an emotional logic. We all know how unpredictable life is. One day we feel at one with God and the next we are struggling to sense his presence. That's part of the danger of relying too much on emotion: we should trust to God's truths instead.

PRAYER

God our Father, guide me into your hope, even when I am surrounded by trouble.

When surrounded by besetting sins

Blessed is he that considereth the poor: the Lord will deliver him in time of trouble... Mine enemies speak evil of me, When shall he die, and his name perish? ... Yea, mine own familiar friend, in whom I trusted, which did eat of my bread, hath lifted up his heel against me. But thou, O Lord, be merciful unto me, and raise me up, that I may requite them.

The first section of the book of Psalms ends with a combination of thanksgiving and pleading to God that neatly sums up many of the concerns that we have seen in these highlights from Psalms 22—41. The psalm plays with generalised observations about God, as well as sharp, individual cries from a specific situation. Again, we have a setting that sounds much like the Christian life, in which we are assured of ultimate victory, though meanwhile the suffering and sin of the world continue.

These enemies in the psalms have been interpreted in a number of ways. It is important to remember that, as this is poetry, they can be different things at the same time and so might not be easily reducible to a single object. They could be a group of people—perhaps a foreign nation at war with the Israelites. They could be people making false accusations in a court against the psalmist, which might explain the anxious tone and assertion of innocence in some psalms. Some have seen the enemies as occult sorcerers, too, while others have associated the troubles of the psalms with physical illness. There is, however, a long and respectable tradition of thinking of the foes also as spiritual ones—sins and troubles that separate us from God.

So, here, it is possible to find a meaning for ourselves by seeing the enemies as our besetting sins. Hence my pride murmurs against me and nearly causes my downfall. The betrayal by a former friend can be both literally true and also like the abilities that I trusted and perhaps felt smug about, which have let me down because I was not using them properly and in God's service.

--------- REFLECTION ---------

Throughout our reading of these psalms, we have found thanksgiving to God coming from the midst of suffering. Can we truly say the same of our own life of faith, or does trouble drive us away from God?

The ideal woman of Proverbs 31

I have very mixed views about this chapter from the book of Proverbs. It used to come round every two years in the old Alternative Service Book cycle of readings in the Church of England, and I would always struggle to take it seriously, finding its portrait of the ideal woman full of bitter irony. Here was the perfect woman, doing all the work (as usual) while the men just sat around (see v. 23). Surely this reinforces the injustice of keeping half the population in a subservient position, making everyone the loser in such a skewed society? There must be more to it than my prejudice, so I am trying to return to the text with a more open mind.

This chapter is the last in the book of Proverbs, which is largely a collection of instructions about how to live wisely. Although it was traditionally attributed to King Solomon, Proverbs is now seen by most scholars as a combination of texts from a number of sources. It was associated with Solomon because he was held up as an example of wisdom and this type of teaching was linked with the royal court. The early chapters of Proverbs (1—9) were probably put together after the later ones and made to form an introduction to them. They consist of parents' instructions to children and descriptions of the idea of wisdom, portrayed as a woman. Chapters 10—31 then take the form of wise sayings and advice.

Proverbs is a type of literature about wisdom, a form that is found in many cultures. Much of it sounds like common sense—folk wisdom that most people would agree with. Consequently, it can sound conventional, even trite: 'He becometh poor that dealeth with a slack hand: but the hand of the diligent maketh rich' (Proverbs 10:4), for example. To modern, cynical ears, it might seem self-consciously pious, perhaps even leading to the sort of smugness of which others accuse religious people. Yet, at its best, this type of wisdom can be inspiring. We shouldn't make the mistake of thinking that the modern world is anti-wisdom. Just think of the vast industry that is modern wisdom-seeking—the rush for qualifications and experts, and magazines and TV shows stuffed with hints and tips. We certainly have a sense that there is wisdom out there, even if now we're not sure where best to find it.

Nothing new under the sun

The words of king Lemuel, the prophecy that his mother taught him.
What, my son? and what, the son of my womb? and what, the son
of my vows? Give not thy strength unto women, nor thy ways to that
which destroyeth kings. It is not for kings, O Lemuel, it is not for
kings to drink wine; nor for princes strong drink.

The chapter begins with the type of advice that runs throughout the
book of Proverbs. It's a warning against the dangers of sex with the
wrong person and of drink. The teaching is attributed to the mother of King
Lemuel, who is not named and is known only as a result of her relationship
to him. Lemuel is otherwise unknown, too, so we can't claim much more
about him. His name survives more today in Jonathan Swift's character,
Lemuel Gulliver, and his celebrated travels.

Queen Mothers do not often figure in the Bible, but scholars have linked
these instructions to manuals for training future kings, particularly in
Egypt. Both the Egyptian and Hebrew traditions of wisdom are concerned
with the responsibilities of rulers to listen to wisdom and avoid bloodshed
and excessive luxury.

As in much of the book of Proverbs, the advice can sound crushingly
obvious. What mother doesn't want to steer her children away from the
wrong sort of sex and booze? Yet we still find it so hard to avoid such
temptations. Dangerous liaisons and overindulgence are fun, of course,
particularly when they have the glamour of being frowned on by others. If
we could solve these problems, we would all be massively better off. In our
age of loutishness, we are hardly in a position to mock traditional wisdom.

There could be two main responses to this. First, we could lapse into
a form of despair, perhaps leading to world-weary cynicism. We haven't
tackled these problems effectively in thousands of years, so what hope is
there for humankind? On the other hand, we could be encouraged as we
can see how much we have in common with our ancestors, that we share
a common humanity under God and are not alone in our search for the
good and the true.

REFLECTION

*Let us be mindful of all those across the globe who are grappling
with the same problems.*

Don't switch off to good advice

It is not for kings to drink wine; nor for princes strong drink: Lest they drink, and forget the law, and pervert the judgment of any of the afflicted. Give strong drink unto him that is ready to perish, and wine unto those that be of heavy hearts. Let him drink, and forget his poverty, and remember his misery no more. Open thy mouth for the dumb in the cause of all such as are appointed to destruction. Open thy mouth, judge righteously, and plead the cause of the poor and needy.

In the second part of this introduction, King Lemuel's mother gives her reasons for steering him away from drink. She goes beyond a basic warning about his having responsibilities to maintain, for she specifically mentions his duty to those suffering most. This sounds very modern ('plead the cause of the poor and needy', v. 9), but of course she is drawing on the same tradition found in so much of the Old Testament—that of a duty towards the unprotected, the widow and orphan (see, for example, Psalm 146:9 and Deuteronomy 14:29).

As we saw at the beginning of this chapter, this might seem like conventional good advice, but we shouldn't use this as an excuse for failing to heed it. It's so easy for such words to pass us by—rather like when we hear familiar passages or prayers in church. We can switch off and stop applying the message to ourselves, as if merely by hearing such words we had actually done something to carry them out. But the challenge to us is still there.

It is more striking that Lemuel's mother sees a positive use for strong drink. It can serve some purpose for 'those that be of heavy hearts' (v. 6), providing the temporary relief of forgetting misery. I'm sure she's not recommending alcohol as a solution to problems, but she can see why people turn to it and doesn't seem to blame them. Surely we can learn something from this? We shouldn't condemn people out of hand, pretending that their sins are utterly foreign to us. It's far too easy to spot motes in others' eyes, forgetting the beams in our own (Matthew 7:3–4; Luke 6:41–42).

PRAYER

Father, thank you for giving me the opportunity to help others.
Grant that I may do so gladly, in the knowledge that we are all sinners.

Pulled in different directions

Who can find a virtuous woman? for her price is far above rubies.
The heart of her husband doth safely trust in her, so that he shall
have no need of spoil. She will do him good and not evil all the
days of her life. She seeketh wool, and flax, and worketh willingly
with her hands. She is like the merchants' ships; she bringeth her
food from afar.

Now we reach the meat of the chapter, the 'ode to a virtuous woman'.
This is written as an acrostic poem, each verse beginning with a different letter of the Hebrew alphabet. In some ways, this praise for the ideal
wife, coming at the very end of Proverbs, sums up the whole book. The
ideal wife can be seen as Wisdom herself—the virtue that is portrayed as
a woman in earlier chapters. In Proverbs 9:1–6, for example, 'Wisdom' is
seen as a woman who builds a house with seven pillars, then invites 'simple' people to eat with her.

There is a sense of a good woman being a gift from God to those around
her (as in Proverbs 18:22; here, at verse 11, her husband does not need
'spoil' or any further gain). This follows on from the advice earlier in the
book about falling in with the right crowd, but it also goes beyond this, for
a good woman can influence the whole household. As we shall see later in
the chapter, her children, those who work for her and the whole community
(including the needy) benefit from her goodness. She sets a virtuous circle
in motion, spurring on those around her to do the right thing.

In these verses, she is praised for providing for the household and being
a good shopper. It reminds me of a cartoon by Posy Simmonds about
the many roles a modern woman has to play. There is 'The Provident
Housewife', laden with supermarket bags; 'The Angel of the Hearth',
furnishing a comfortable home; and even 'The Strumpet of the Boudoir',
catering for her husband's needs. The point, of course, is that a woman
is expected to be all these things, even if she ends up exhausted by being
pulled in different directions.

--- **REFLECTION** ---

*Think about your family, friends, colleagues and fellow worshippers at church.
How much do we really know about the various tasks they do
and the pressures on them?*

The biblical businesswoman

She riseth also while it is yet night, and giveth meat to her household,
and a portion to her maidens. She considereth a field, and buyeth it:
with the fruit of her hands she planteth a vineyard. She girdeth her
loins with strength, and strengtheneth her arms. She perceiveth that
her merchandise is good: her candle goeth not out by night.

These verses show the ideal woman not just as wife, mother and domestic goddess, but as an employer and businesswoman. She goes beyond the private household sphere and out into property development and trading. She's certainly no clueless trophy wife, indulging herself with shopping and pampering (as seems to be an ideal for some people now).

It makes me wonder why we haven't drawn on this passage more to justify women working outside the home. Here is a patriarchal voice praising a woman who prospers in a man's world of business. She is capable, efficient and wise. Men could learn a great deal from her, too.

As we saw with the previous reading (vv. 10–14), this ideal woman is also frighteningly up to date. She is like many women throughout the world who hold down jobs as well as running a household. At the same time, she shares much with women from poorer countries, who have always done hard physical labour (v. 17). There is a statistic from a United Nations report about how women do nearly two-thirds of the world's work. The end of it is chilling: women receive one-tenth of the world's income and own less than one-hundreth of its property.

We don't seem to have made much progress in the 2500 or so years since Proverbs was composed. Women are exploited in rich and poor countries alike. Sometimes, it's our own fault: we don't always ask for help with domestic tasks or train our children to do them, and often we choose to work for money to maintain ever-higher standards of living or luxuries, such as larger homes. However, women want to provide for their children as best they can and very often have no choice but to work hard. Perhaps this passage provides a justification for such pressures and desires, and perhaps it offers a blessing for our labours, which so often seem to be taken for granted.

--- **PRAYER** ---

*Father, thank you for the women who keep the world going by virtue of their
hard work. Grant that they may find you and your blessings.*

Generosity doesn't rule out elegance

She layeth her hands to the spindle, and her hands hold the distaff.
She stretcheth out her hand to the poor; yea, she reacheth forth her
hands to the needy. She is not afraid of the snow for her household:
for all her household are clothed with scarlet. She maketh herself
coverings of tapestry; her clothing is silk and purple.

Is there no end to this woman's perfection? I'm glad of verse 20, empha-
sising her generosity to the needy. Without this, she could seem self-
serving, looking only to herself and her own. The idea of almsgiving is yet
another of the good works praised in the book of Proverbs that can become
so familiar that often we pay only lip-service to it.

Fundraisers sometimes say that their job is a matter of persuading people that, first, the cause is deserving and, second, they really can afford
to give. We all seem to think it's someone else's job to keep the Church
going, when many of us could give more if we wanted to. We shouldn't
need to have our arms twisted. God has given us everything, so it should
be part of our joyful response: 'All things come from you, and of your own
do we give you', as we say in many churches at the offertory. Just think
of the widow's mite (Mark 12:41–44): Jesus praises her for pouring out
everything she had.

For many of us, including our ideal woman, there is something left after
our generosity. The 'silk and purple' suggests opulence and dignified taste
(perhaps Armani, rather than Versace), but it doesn't say that such luxury is
wicked in itself. Rather, it seems to be the woman's reward for her diligence.
We needn't be afraid of elegance: we don't have to sacrifice everything to a
crabbed sense of duty.

Sometimes people who argue for uglification and the neglect of God's
gifts of beauty are like Judas, who suggested that Mary's expensive perfume
was wasted on Jesus: she should have sold it and given the money to the
poor, he said (John 12:5–6). Sometimes when we do this, like Judas, we are
hiding greater sins and perhaps wouldn't give the cash to charity anyway.
When faced with a street charity collection, I've caught myself thinking,
'I'm not giving to that half-worthy cause: my precious money will go further
in poorer countries,' but then I don't get round to giving it to the poorer
countries, either.

--- **PRAYER** ---

Lord God of abundant life, help me to be a cheerful giver.

Dedication or exploitation?

Her husband is known in the gates, when he sitteth among the elders of the land. She maketh fine linen, and selleth it; and delivereth girdles unto the merchant. Strength and honour are her clothing; and she shall rejoice in time to come. She openeth her mouth with wisdom; and in her tongue is the law of kindness. She looketh well to the ways of her household, and eateth not the bread of idleness.

Now verse 23 is the one that really riles me. All this time the ideal woman has been beavering away, her husband is simply sitting with the elders. It looks as if she does the work and he just has a good time chatting.

This might not be the whole story: perhaps the husband does other things, too. Somehow his idleness seems horribly credible, however. Often, at work, I've been in touch with people and it has become clear that the boss (usually male) seems to spend most of his time going to meetings and looking important, as in these verses, while his subordinates (usually female) are the ones who really get the job done.

What can we do about our sense of the injustice of this situation? As we found with verses 15–18, we can speak up for a fairer sharing of tasks, both personally and on a global scale. We don't have to be strident about it, but to try to see the situation from a more balanced perspective and represent our own and others' needs. We're all God's children, equally loved and deserving of respect.

We can learn something, too, from our ideal woman, in her 'strength and honour' and 'wisdom', as well as the wonderful phrase 'in her tongue is the law of kindness' (vv. 25–26). She gets satisfaction from jobs well done. As with her giving to the poor, she goes further than mere efficiency in her generosity and adherence to standards of kindness. We would all be better off if we saw such fellow-feeling with others as a sort of law. Perhaps she is like the people who responded to a survey by the Chartered Institute of Personnel and Development about long working hours, who said that they enjoyed what they did and actually chose to work for longer. I've always found it satisfying to do a task thoroughly, even if I've sometimes felt exploited: I get more out of putting more in.

PRAYER

*Father, help us to respond with kindness, but fairness,
when we see injustices in your world.*

A vision of wisdom

Her children arise up, and call her blessed; her husband also, and he praiseth her. Many daughters have done virtuously, but thou excellest them all. Favour is deceitful, and beauty is vain: but a woman that feareth the Lord, she shall be praised. Give her of the fruit of her hands; and let her own works praise her in the gates.

This chapter, and with it the whole book of Proverbs, ends with a reflection on the theme of justice, as seen in the previous reading. The hardworking woman should share in the benefits she has created and be acknowledged publicly, in the city gates—the place where men gather, away from women's usual domestic domain (v. 31).

This is more than she might have hoped for in such a society. We must all know people who work hard, both women and men, who are not given a word of encouragement; but here, praise flows from the whole family. Quite right, too, was my initial reaction. It's all very well for her children and husband to arise up and call her blessed, but do they actually help her out with the work? But perhaps I'm being too cynical in thinking that they don't, although they haven't been mentioned in connection with any of her tasks.

The penultimate verse contains the only mention of God in this 22-verse poem. The highest praise a husband can give to the ideal wife is to say that she 'feareth the Lord'. This neatly brings the book of Proverbs back to its beginning, as its opening told how 'The fear of the Lord is the beginning of knowledge' (1:7). Earlier chapters described wisdom, but here she is in the person of a wife, mother, homemaker and businesswoman. She has true knowledge, which she puts into practice.

This idea sets the perfect woman into context, in terms of God's love for us all. The woman can see the truth of God's lovingkindness, and her actions spring from this core of her being. She may be only an imaginary idea, but that shouldn't stop us from being inspired by the vision she sets before us. It's a vision of personal integrity, wholehearted love for others and dedicated work to bring good to people. We should go and do likewise.

REFLECTION

What can I do today to respond to this ideal and build up God's kingdom?

Lamentations: how it feels to grieve

The book of Lamentations consists of outpourings of grief about the destruction of Jerusalem and the sufferings of its (or 'her', as the city is portrayed as a woman) once-proud people. The laments, though, are not just howls of inarticulate pain: they try to make sense of what has happened, and what it says about God. This is why they are worth reading now. They offer an unflinchingly honest insight into how it feels to be brought low. They deal with the destruction of a whole society. In this, they offer parallels with the Holocaust and more recent genocide in Rwanda and Bosnia. The savage twist here, though, is that the sufferer has no one to blame but herself. God has brought about this disaster because of sin.

Although Lamentations is traditionally associated with the prophet Jeremiah, scholars no longer link it with him. The book was probably ascribed to him to make it seem more significant, but no one knows who wrote it. It was probably compiled after the fall of Jerusalem to the Babylonians and the destruction of the temple in 587BC. Then, most of the city's people were taken as prisoners to Babylon, leaving a few to compose these laments.

The book's handling of suffering gives it much in common with the Psalms. Like them, these laments are written in poetry, and the KJV draws this out beautifully, with a direct and telling power of its own. Often they use complex structures, such as the acrostic, in which each verse begins with a different letter of the Hebrew alphabet.

Like much reflection on grief, the book veers from despair to hope and back to despair again. It reflects the moods of the writer, who goes over the same ground again and again, trying to come to terms with the disaster. In this, Lamentations is a classic depiction of our common response to grief and also one of the earliest works in the tradition of writing about loss. From extended meditations, such as Tennyson's long series of poems, *In Memoriam* (1850), to modern approaches, such as C.S. Lewis' *A Grief Observed* (1961), great writers have wrestled with bereavement. In doing so, they have helped the rest of us realise that we are not alone in our losses— whether of friends and family in death, or home, status, youth or other things that define us. I've found myself referring to *In Memoriam* several times in these notes on Lamentations, as it captures the tone of anguish, regret and questioning about why losses happen, and how on earth we might cope with them.

Crying in the night

How doth the city sit solitary, that was full of people! how is she become as a widow! she that was great among the nations, and princess among the provinces, how is she become tributary! She weepeth sore in the night, and her tears are on her cheeks: among all her lovers she hath none to comfort her: all her friends have dealt treacherously with her, they are become her enemies.

The book of Lamentations begins as it means to go on—grieving for the disaster that has come upon the once-proud city of Jerusalem. There is a healthy desire to acknowledge the full horror rather than attempt to sweep it under the carpet. The time for turning to the future will come later, but, for now, it is appropriate to grieve.

So Lamentations piles up the images of suffering—loneliness, betrayal, weeping—to create a vivid picture of pain. Yet all this is done without the specific details of what exactly caused the disaster. The book dwells on only part of the story and we never really see the full picture. Here, it's the effect on people that matters, not a precise chronicle of what brought it all about.

In these opening verses, we are shown Jerusalem as a widow: lonely, deserted and forced into servitude (and in a society in which this state was desperate, because a widow had no one to provide or care for her). The writer contemplates her from a distance in verse 1 before zooming in to focus more closely on her inner turmoil. She has been betrayed by those she should have been able to turn to for help.

The picture of someone crying in the night, on their own, is a powerful one: 'she weepeth sore' encapsulates so much. The Psalms draw on it (Psalms 6:6 and 42:3 for example: the former says, 'all the night make I my bed to swim'), as does Tennyson in *In Memoriam* (see below). Every one of us has cried alone in the night, whether we admit it or not: we can each think about why and when. The image calls on us to acknowledge that there are times when we all share in the sense of such utter loss.

--- REFLECTION ---

... but what am I?
An infant crying in the night:
An infant crying for the light:
And with no language but a cry.

Alfred, Lord Tennyson, *In Memoriam*

— LAMENTATIONS 1:3–5 (ABRIDGED) —

Look at what your sins do

Judah... findeth no rest: all her persecutors overtook her between the straits. The ways of Zion do mourn, because none come to the solemn feasts: all her gates are desolate: her priests sigh, her virgins are afflicted, and she is in bitterness. Her adversaries are the chief, her enemies prosper; for the Lord hath afflicted her for the multitude of her transgressions.

Now the writer sketches just part of what has happened. The nation has been forced into exile, 'into captivity'; the people have been driven out of their homes. It is thought that this refers to the fall of Jerusalem in 587BC, when the first temple was destroyed and the Babylonians took away the Israelites as prisoners. Those who were left behind met on the site of the temple to mourn, and the book of Lamentations was recited at such gatherings.

This is why the words commemorate the disaster. They form part of the people's determination to remember. The Israelites need to recall the moment of suffering both to bind together their community in a common experience and to avoid complacency, fatalism and laziness. They want to draw on this time of suffering, to use what they have learnt so that it won't happen again.

Why has this happened? The Lord has punished Israel (v. 5a). If her people had not sinned, God would not have brought this on them. We're not talking about undeserved suffering here; this isn't the affliction of a righteous man like Job. This is that disaster for which we know we are to blame, at least to some extent—and, as with our lonely crying in the night, we have all been there.

We need to be careful here, though. We need to remember that the rain falls alike on the righteous and the unrighteous (Matthew 5:45), and that much suffering doesn't happen as a direct result of sin—as Jesus said about those who died beneath the Tower of Siloam (Luke 13:4–5). We shouldn't allow ourselves to wallow in a generalised sense of guilt. Instead, we could begin by examining our specific faults and tracing where they have brought grief to others.

REFLECTION

'If we confess our sins, he is faithful and just to forgive us our sins, and to cleanse us from all unrighteousness' (1 John 1:9).

The pain of public mockery

Jerusalem remembered in the days of her affliction and of her miseries all her pleasant things that she had in the days of old, when her people fell into the hand of the enemy, and none did help her: the adversaries saw her, and did mock at her sabbaths. Jerusalem hath grievously sinned; therefore she is removed: all that honoured her despise her, because they have seen her nakedness... O Lord, behold my affliction: for the enemy hath magnified himself.

Having established that the Israelites must bear some responsibility for the disaster that has struck them, the author goes into further detail about their afflictions. One of the aspects that particularly twists the knife is the public humiliation. This is not a private grief that can be mourned behind closed doors. The enemies of Zion are delighted to be able to gloat over her. The KJV's 'the enemy hath magnified himself' is translated elsewhere 'the enemy has triumphed' (NIV, NRSV).

This is particularly painful for a proud nation. We can imagine their having felt smug, assuming that God was on their side, thinking themselves superior to those around them, rather like some other nations in more recent centuries. But, before we indulge our own condescension (of course, we're not like that), we need to examine our consciences. Do I count my blessings as undeserved grace or is there a sneaking suspicion that they are a reward for some supposed virtue?

Some of us might enjoy drawing facile parallels between the Israelites' lordly behaviour and that of the United States in its recent foreign policy. It's not as simple as that, however: as we considered in a previous reading, shouldn't we look at the beam in our own eye (Matthew 7:3–5)?

The suffering referred to here is portrayed as a direct result of Zion's sin. We can all bring this kind of trouble on ourselves, and then we have to face up to the consequences of our actions. It's not surprising that others mock, but perhaps this cruel treatment is what we need to jolt us back to our senses.

To deal with this, surely we have to return to the Lord, as the writer starts to do here. We need to face up to and confess our sin, make reparation where possible, and resolve to mend our ways. Easier said than done, but it does offer a way back.

--- **PRAYER** ---

Father, help me to acknowledge my sins and turn back to you.

Is it nothing to you?

All her people sigh, they seek bread; they have given their pleasant things for meat to relieve the soul: see, O Lord, and consider; for I am become vile. Is it nothing to you, all ye that pass by? behold, and see if there be any sorrow like unto my sorrow, which is done unto me, wherewith the Lord hath afflicted me in the day of his fierce anger. From above hath he sent fire into my bones, and it prevaileth against them: he hath spread a net for my feet, he hath turned me back: he hath made me desolate and faint all the day. The yoke of my transgressions is bound by his hand: they are wreathed, and come up upon my neck: he hath made my strength to fall, the Lord hath delivered me into their hands, from whom I am not able to rise up.

The first part of verse 12 has gained a wider currency by its use in Holy Week services. The compilers of the services apply the verse to Jesus as he addresses those witnessing the crucifixion: 'See if there be any sorrow like unto my sorrow.'

In that context, the words speak powerfully of the indifference towards what Jesus is going through on our behalf. It's not good enough just to accuse others of ignoring what God is doing. We all share in that refusal to acknowledge God, at least some of the time.

Once I was at a Good Friday service where this was acted out, in a way that reflected no credit on the Church. 'Is it nothing to you, all you who pass by?' a priest harangued those who were walking through the church, which was a big tourist destination. We in the congregation could feel self-righteous—we had come for the service—and those others were the bad ones, passing by on the other side. Actually, I don't think it was for any of us to judge their intentions: most of them were respectful of the building and its purpose.

This approach of applying the verses to Jesus can help us to realise the consequences of sin. It is human pride, greed and jealousy that have put Jesus on the cross. It takes such extremity of suffering to make us see what is wrong and, we hope, jolt us out of our complacency.

--- **PRAYER** ---

Father, help me to see where sin leads and to turn away from it,
towards your love.

Why we all need to mourn

The Lord hath trodden under foot all my mighty men in the midst of me: he hath called an assembly against me to crush my young men: the Lord hath trodden the virgin, the daughter of Judah, as in a winepress. For these things I weep; mine eye, mine eye runneth down with water, because the comforter that should relieve my soul is far from me: my children are desolate, because the enemy prevailed.

―――――――――――

The book of Lamentations marks a national disaster, similar to the World Wars of the 20th century: many have died (see Lamentations 2:21, though the details are confused) and life will never be the same again.

When war veterans are interviewed, so often they say that they want to recall fallen comrades rather than to celebrate victory. Of course, they know better than the rest of us about the hollowness of military triumph. The old soldiers want to remember and to mourn. The whole book of Lamentations marks (celebrates, even) this desire and, in a way, blesses it. We shouldn't just rush on and ignore the past. We need to commemorate it, to remember what happened, and try to learn from it.

Mourning isn't something that is marked in modern culture. It's easy to criticise the heavy Victorian conventions, such as those that prescribed clothes of deepest black for a year, but at least there was some structure, which people could cling to in their grief. It gave a framework that mapped out its stages. They didn't ignore the fact of death or hustle people back to jollity before they were ready, or become embarrassed and try to avoid bereaved people, as we sometimes do today.

We should mourn the losses in our society as well as our personal griefs. When we see others, and ourselves, turning away from God, it is sad: something in us has died. At his enthronement as Archbishop of Canterbury in 2003, Dr Rowan Williams spoke of 'a real hunger and thirst to see God's image, the destiny of human beings to become God's sons and daughters' and 'a real grief and fear... if this does not come to light'.

――――――――― REFLECTION ―――――――――

'The Church has to warn and to lament, as well as to comfort.'
Archbishop Rowan Williams (enthronement sermon, 2003)

Entering the darkness

The Lord hath cast off his altar, he hath abhorred his sanctuary, he hath given up into the hand of the enemy the walls of her palaces; they have made a noise in the house of the Lord, as in the day of a solemn feast... The law is no more; her prophets also find no vision from the Lord. The elders of the daughter of Zion sit upon the ground, and keep silence: they have cast up dust upon their heads; they have girded themselves with sackcloth... Mine eyes do fail with tears, my bowels are troubled, my liver is poured upon the earth, for the destruction of the daughter of my people; because the children and the sucklings swoon in the streets of the city.

Moving on from the commemoration of grief in the previous reading, these verses form part of the lessons read at the service of Tenebrae in Holy Week. The word *tenebrae* means 'darkness' and the service was, and is still, held to look ahead to the suffering of the cross. The destruction of the holy city is like the destruction of all the disciples' hopes and plans, as well as the destruction of Jesus' life. There is a parallel sense of utter desolation—even of being abandoned by God ('her prophets also find no vision from the Lord', v. 9b).

The service of Tenebrae has three unique aspects. The first is the special readings from Lamentations, including these verses. The second is the dramatic ritual of snuffing out candles, one by one, at the end of each reading from the Psalms. After all the candles are extinguished, the people are left in darkness. Then comes the third aspect: in the dark church, both congregation and ministers bang the pews. This harsh clatter is thought to recall the scourging of Jesus by the Roman soldiers.

You can imagine the combination of these words about ruins with the gradually darkening building, and then the sudden, rough noise. The sights and sounds take you further into the experience, and you get a sense of how serious such mourning is.

Sometimes we need to enter into the depths to enlarge our sympathies and gain an insight into an experience of loss.

PRAYER

Father, fill us with imaginative sympathy for our suffering brothers and sisters. Help us to break through the loneliness of grief to reach out to others.

Return to the Lord your God

They say to their mothers, Where is corn and wine? when they swooned as the wounded in the streets of the city, when their soul was poured out into their mothers' bosom... for thy breach is great like the sea: who can heal thee? Thy prophets have seen vain and foolish things for thee: and they have not discovered thine iniquity, to turn away thy captivity... All that pass by clap their hands at thee; they hiss and wag their head at the daughter of Jerusalem, saying, Is this the city that men call The perfection of beauty, The joy of the whole earth?

In the previous reading, we saw how Lamentations is used in the service of Tenebrae. Often the words are sung, but with a crucial addition—one that points to the purpose of Zion's suffering.

This is the second of the passages read at that service. But, at the end of each set of verses, the compilers added some words adapted from Hosea 14:1: 'Jerusalem, Jerusalem, return to the Lord your God.' As we saw in Lamentations 1:7–9, turning to God is what it is all about. In the weeping and hunger, we see the consequences of sin as the innocent suffer (v. 12). Few sights are more heartrending than children crying from hunger and the distress of mothers who cannot help them.

The people need to turn back to the Lord. Over the course of the Tenebrae service, this becomes a refrain, interacting with the details of the people's griefs. All their woes point back to this need. I have been at services where the words have been sung like this. The haunting chorus lingers long in the memory. It also feels as if it's addressed to each of us personally. This is the Lord your God. There is no mistaking the emotional pull, especially in music such as the setting by Thomas Tallis. There, musical colouring, dissonance and contrast dramatise the laments.

As we travel deeper into the grief, verse 14 points up the paradox of our need to face the ugly facts about our faults. Platitudes from false prophets ('vain and foolish things', the KJV says neatly) only make it worse: these are hollow bogus-religious types who are relentlessly cheery and won't face the reality of sin and its consequences. It is only by descending to the depths that we can start again. Music, drama and poetry can sometimes help by drawing us into the experience in a fresh way, offering others' insights.

--- **PRAYER** ---

Turn me back to you, Lord.

Good, the final goal of ill

Arise, cry out in the night: in the beginning of the watches pour out thine heart like water before the face of the Lord: lift up thy hands toward him for the life of thy young children, that faint for hunger in the top of every street... The young and the old lie on the ground in the streets: my virgins and my young men are fallen by the sword; thou hast slain them in the day of thine anger; thou hast killed, and not pitied. Thou hast called as in a solemn day my terrors round about, so that in the day of the Lord's anger none escaped nor remained: those that I have swaddled and brought up hath mine enemy consumed.

Lamentations offers us a scene of complete destruction. It's the slaughter that matters: the loss of people—rather than buildings, possessions, or pride—that needs to be mourned. As with so much of the suffering of war, it's the waste that hits hardest. All the investment of effort and hope has come to nothing: 'those that I have swaddled and brought up hath mine enemy consumed' (v. 22: 'consumed' can also be translated 'destroyed' here).

This is surely one of the greatest fears of those who are left behind to mourn. As Tennyson wrote in *In Memoriam*, which is part tribute and part reflection on grief, composed after the death of his closest friend:

Oh yet we trust that somehow good
Will be the final goal of ill...

That not one life shall be destroyed,
Or cast as rubbish to the void,
When God hath made the pile complete.

Even if hopes are only faint, we can look to the passing of time and cling on in faith. As Tennyson continues:

I can but trust that good shall fall
At last—far off—at last, to all,
And every winter change to spring.

We can hold these two truths in mind as we recall those who have died. First, the need we have noted throughout Lamentations to grieve and to remember; and second, the need to salvage what good we can from the bad, to create a chance for better things.

REFLECTION

Father, help us to be the ones to prove that others' sacrifices have not been in vain. Help us to add to the good for those we meet today.

Open to God

I am the man that hath seen affliction by the rod of his wrath. He hath led me, and brought me into darkness, but not into light. Surely against me is he turned; he turneth his hand against me all the day. My flesh and my skin hath he made old; he hath broken my bones. He hath builded against me, and compassed me with gall and travail.

He hath set me in dark places, as they that be dead of old.

Here, near the middle of the book, the focus shifts to an individual, perhaps a representative of the people or the voice of the writer, in a complex piece of Hebrew poetry. He feels utterly wrecked, without any let-up (v. 3), physically (v. 4) and spiritually ('compassed me with gall and travail', v. 5). It reminds me of Gerard Manley Hopkins' poem that begins 'No worst, there is none. Pitched past pitch of grief…'.

As in many of the Psalms (22 and 42, for example), sometimes we need to anatomise what is wrong: to explore it and find a name for our trouble, rather than subsisting on a generalised sense of misery and nameless dread. When we're ill, it's a great relief when we get a diagnosis that gives a name to our problem, even if it's a terrible one—better that than the fear of uncertainty.

Sometimes, too, it's helpful to struggle to find exact words for our wounds, rather than an inarticulate howl of pain. This was one of Tennyson's motivations for writing about his loss in *In Memoriam*:

But, for the unquiet heart and brain,
　A use in measured language lies;
　The sad mechanic exercise,
Like dull narcotics, numbing pain.

However much we are told that God cherishes such honesty, though, it can be hard to persuade ourselves to let go and trust him with the truth of our feelings. We would rather nurse those grudges and let them fester than lay them open to his healing love. It's as if we don't really believe that he will still love us if we expose ourselves before him. But think for a moment: we're talking about God, our loving Father. Surely he wants us to turn to him, whatever our mood.

--- **REFLECTION** ---

Think about what you are hiding from God today.

Great is thy faithfulness

Remembering mine affliction and my misery, the wormwood and the gall. My soul hath them still in remembrance, and is humbled in me. This I recall to my mind, therefore have I hope. It is of the Lord's mercies that we are not consumed, because his compassions fail not. They are new every morning: great is thy faithfulness. The Lord is my portion, saith my soul; therefore will I hope in him. The Lord is good unto them that wait for him, to the soul that seeketh him.

Just as the miseries are piling up, grief upon grief, so that you wonder whether things could get any worse, there is a sudden glimmer of hope, which builds into the only sustained passage of positive writing in the whole book of Lamentations. Without warning, the thought of love bursts into the narrator's consciousness: here comes the idea of God's mercies, which never end.

The result is a sense of renewal, coming like rain on parched ground. We drink it up eagerly. Of course, it's all the more potent after such a drought of misery. But doesn't hope often spring up like this, seemingly out of nowhere? Are there times you can remember when everything had been grim and desperate, when you got through life somehow, but realised only when looking back how terrible it had been? Then, perhaps undramatically, but still distinctly, the situation began to seem different. One day there might have been a little movement and, after that, things started to improve.

Such turns are surely the work of the Holy Spirit, working in us for good. We may change and drift away, but God is always waiting for us ('new every morning', vv. 22–23), like the father in the story of the prodigal son (Luke 15:11–32). George Herbert expresses this neatly in 'The Flower', a poem that has reached out to many at times of bereavement, including the late Queen Mother, BRF's former patron. She thanked someone who had sent her the words below, after the death of her husband, George VI, saying how moving and helpful she had found them.

--- REFLECTION ---

How fresh, O Lord, how sweet and clean
Are thy returns! ev'n as the flowers in spring...
Grief melts away
Like snow in May,
As if there were no such cold thing.
George Herbert, 'The Flower' (1633)

Return to the Lord without fear

Let us search and try our ways, and turn again to the Lord. Let us lift up our heart with our hands unto God in the heavens... Waters flowed over mine head; then I said, I am cut off. I called upon thy name, O Lord, out of the low dungeon. Thou hast heard my voice: hide not thine ear at my breathing, at my cry. Thou drewest near in the day that I called upon thee: thou saidst, Fear not. O Lord, thou hast pleaded the causes of my soul; thou hast redeemed my life.

At last, the writer gives us something we can actually do. For the first time in this chapter, it is 'us' who can act, rather than an isolated individual. He suggests practical action for us to get on with, which will help to remedy this disaster. We need to look at ourselves honestly and turn to God (vv. 40–41).

Most of us have surely had moments when we felt the waters closing over us (v. 54). It is at this precise moment that we can call on the Lord. He will respond. Here, as elsewhere in scripture (Isaiah 41:10 or Luke 1:30, for example), the message is simple: 'Fear not.' Sometimes we're so locked into fear that we don't know what we're afraid of any more. But God will reassure us—not in any childish, comfort-blanket sense, but with the truth and justice suggested by God's having 'pleaded the causes of my soul' (v. 58).

As I've already mentioned, once I worked in a very unhappy place, where the people at the middle and bottom of the hierarchy felt let down by those at the top: they were treated as worthless. In order to deal with the situation, some of us looked to passages in the Old Testament about God's justice for his people. We weren't after special favours, only fairness. Those who are in the depths can look to God's judgment for vindication.

Whatever the world's injustices, God will be the judge in the end. Yet, paradoxically, that does not let us off the hook: we can't just leave it to God to sort out in heaven (as some critics of religion accuse us of doing). The idea of God's justice should make us hunger for right to prevail now, for all his children.

--- **REFLECTION** ---

'Blessed are they which do hunger and thirst after righteousness:
for they shall be filled' (Matthew 5:6).

Facing the consequences of sin (again)

They that did feed delicately are desolate in the streets: they that were brought up in scarlet embrace dunghills... For the sins of her prophets, and the iniquities of her priests, that have shed the blood of the just in the midst of her, They have wandered as blind men in the streets, they have polluted themselves with blood, so that men could not touch their garments. They cried unto them, Depart ye; it is unclean; depart, depart, touch not: when they fled away and wandered, they said among the heathen, They shall no more sojourn there. The anger of the Lord hath divided them; he will no more regard them.

These verses offer some of the book's most striking images of the degradation that has fallen on Jerusalem. Those who were once privileged, those brought up in scarlet and the priests—these people are now despised.

The picture from verse 5 of people who had been rich now clinging to dunghills is a powerful one: 'feed delicately' conjures up a vivid picture of picky indulgence. It reminds me of a photo from a history book we had at school, which showed a Russian princess, after the 1917 Revolution, working as a waitress in Paris. Of course, it seems desperately sad when people are deprived of what they once enjoyed. Your heart goes out to them—even if you suspect that they might have been spoilt rotten before disaster struck.

One response is to think that they didn't deserve all this, but, at least with the priests, the implication is that those who are suffering must bear the responsibility for it, and it is they who have brought these horrors on the whole city (it was 'for the sins of her prophets, and the iniquities of her priests', v. 13). These prophets and priests must face up to the consequences of their actions. In such a situation, our gut response is to say, 'It's not my fault'; to refuse to believe that our actions (or inaction) could affect anyone else, let alone hurt them. Surely we can carry on in our own sweet way, doing just what we want without any regard for others? No, actually. We're not islands; we depend on each other. We're finding out how true this is in many different ways—from the pollution caused by our cars to the products we buy that are produced by exploiting people.

PRAYER

Father, forgive us our trespasses and those who trespass against us.

We each make an impact

Our persecutors are swifter than the eagles of the heaven: they pursued us upon the mountains, they laid wait for us in the wilderness. The breath of our nostrils, the anointed of the Lord, was taken in their pits… Rejoice and be glad, O daughter of Edom, that dwellest in the land of Uz; the cup also shall pass through unto thee: thou shalt be drunken, and shalt make thyself naked. The punishment of thine iniquity is accomplished, O daughter of Zion; he will no more carry thee away into captivity: he will visit thine iniquity, O daughter of Edom; he will discover thy sins.

Following on from the previous reading, we hear more about God's anger being given full vent because of sins. In a way, the whole of Lamentations demonstrates the struggle to come to terms with this fact—that sins have consequences. The writer pours out these details of agony, and still can't quite comprehend what has happened and why.

As so often, we can see this more clearly in the sins of others. So it's often reported that thieves have little sense that what they are doing really causes harm. We're told that they (so different from us, we might think) don't realise that people will have much more than their easily replaceable property damaged in a burglary, and that the impact on their lives can be huge. Often, when offenders are encouraged to meet their victims, they develop a fuller sense of what they have done. We might think ourselves superior, but do we truly realise the effects of our actions?

It seems hard to believe, but we have power and influence over others every time we do such ordinary things as shopping. And, of course, in the West, we have more power than most of the rest of the world's population. Like the people of Jerusalem, we have to face up to the consequences of what we do. If they had done so, they could have avoided the destruction that fell on them. Many believe that our lifestyles are bringing on a similar destruction—that of the earth in an environmental catastrophe—and that we shall have only ourselves to blame.

REFLECTION

Can I direct some of my choices, my spending of time and money,
to have a positive impact on others today?

Restore us to yourself, O Lord

The crown is fallen from our head: woe unto us, that we have sinned!
For this our heart is faint; for these things our eyes are dim. Because
of the mountain of Zion, which is desolate, the foxes walk upon it.
Thou, O Lord, remainest for ever; thy throne from generation to
generation. Wherefore dost thou forget us for ever, and forsake us so
long time? Turn thou us unto thee, O Lord, and we shall be turned;
renew our days as of old. But thou hast utterly rejected us; thou art
very wroth against us.

The final chapter of this long lament piles on more of the now-familiar
details of suffering. The last few verses here, however, point to the reason behind it: 'we have sinned!' (v. 16).

Near the end, there is a turning back to the Lord (v. 19). There is a sense
that if the people put God first, seeking his kingdom and righteousness,
then everything will fall into place (v. 21). Yet this insight is fleeting, and
the book ends on an uncertain note.

This writer should trust his penultimate judgment—that faith in God
will enable him and the whole community to rebuild. This is the foundation they need, but, as so many of us find, it can be hard to believe it. We
know God loves us and holds out the promise of a more abundant life, but
we are reluctant to trust him. God is our loving Father, looking out for our
return and eager to shower us with gifts. Yet we prefer to stay cosily in our
own sins, like a pig in muck.

The anxiety in these last verses shows how deeply the writer is mired in
fear. We can see he is wrong. We know that perfect love drives out all fear
(1 John 4:18), but how often do we apply it to our own situation? Why are
we so afraid of belonging to God?

We are left with this chilling example of the need to commit ourselves to
God, so that we don't descend into selfish sin or isolated fear. Sometimes
we need to abandon the fastidiousness we acquire over the years, and recall
the enthusiasm to reach beyond ourselves.

REFLECTION

… Do not let me hear
Of the wisdom of old men, but rather of their folly,
Their fear of fear and frenzy, their fear of possession,
Of belonging to another, or to others, or to God.

T.S. Eliot, *East Coker* (1940)

INTRODUCTION

The nativity as seen by poets and painters

After the excited waiting of Advent and the celebrations of the non-churchy world (the carol services and parties being mostly finished by about 20 December), comes the real thing—Christmas.

The Bible readings are so familiar, hardly containing an unknown or previously unheard word, that many of us are in danger of letting it all wash over us. It's so easy to be swept along into merely going through the motions, while perhaps enjoying the odd warm glow stealing over us at the most emotive moments.

These are Christmas readings with reference to relevant poetry and paintings. They can give fresh insights and unusual angles, which might mitigate overfamiliarity, but the variety of viewpoints they give us also emphasises that others have struggled with this before, and have come up with different approaches. Others have tried to get beyond the wrappings of the season and search for the meaning.

In comparison with these (usually) older voices, our time seems to get stuck in the human dimension of Christmas. We appear reluctant to move beyond the sweet baby and homely shepherds. It's true that their appeal is immediate and they are important. One of the most wonderful aspects of Christmas is the way that the down-to-earth human detail is drawn into God's plan of salvation.

Yet the artistic material from the past does seem more interested in theology, in the significance of the story's details, rather than just the human tale (though perhaps it is just that the more thoughtful pieces have survived). Perhaps, also, we're ignorant of theology and fight shy of the meaning. So we might notice only the baby Jesus crying like any other small child, showing the touching vulnerability of his humanity, while poets (as we shall see in the reading from Matthew 2) see him weeping for the sins of the world, and thus draw out the wider significance of the incarnation.

Perhaps we retreat into the merely human side because meaning worries us. It could be difficult to understand, so we don't like to explore too deeply in case we get it wrong—as if we're more afraid of being wrong than of making the effort to think. Perhaps we're anxious because it might make demands on our lives.

But Jesus comes to earth for us and, among other things, his coming means that we need to live differently.

Recognition from the womb

And Mary arose in those days, and went into the hill country with haste, into a city of Judah; And entered into the house of Zacharias, and saluted Elisabeth. And it came to pass, that, when Elisabeth heard the salutation of Mary, the babe leaped in her womb; and Elisabeth was filled with the Holy Ghost: And she spake out with a loud voice, and said, Blessed art thou among women, and blessed is the fruit of thy womb. And whence is this to me, that the mother of my Lord should come to me? For, lo, as soon as the voice of thy salutation sounded in mine ears, the babe leaped in my womb for joy.

The scene isn't hard to imagine: two pregnant women meeting one another. It could be comic—two fat ladies bumping their bumps—but the usual impression from artists is one of warm female fellowship. In Ghirlandaio's fresco in S. Maria Novella, Florence, as well as many carvings and stained-glass windows, Mary and Elizabeth are reaching out to each other. The simple outline of their arms communicates a message of tender support.

Yet this isn't a cosy antenatal class. After the initial greeting, Elizabeth doesn't bother with compliments about Mary blooming. 'Blessed are you,' she says, and looks to the wider consequences. Mary isn't just a member of Elizabeth's extended family; she is now the most important woman on earth, 'the mother of my Lord'. Elizabeth realises that this visit isn't just about solidarity: it is an honour. 'And whence is this to me…?' can also be translated, 'Why has this happened to me?' It carries a sense of wonder.

Mary has acquired this great status by her decision in favour of God and her belief in him. There are stories from the Eastern Orthodox Christian tradition that the angel Gabriel approached other women before Mary. They said no, just as she could have done.

Although this visitation scene can be portrayed as a simple meeting, here it is weighed with cosmic significance. For the first time, someone acknowledges the meaning of these events. The Lord is coming—Elizabeth and her son John, though still a foetus, recognise it. As with the whole Christmas story, the human and divine are woven together so closely that they can't be separated. Mary might be grateful for the boost and the reassurance Elizabeth gives (as most pregnant women are, as far as I remember). But she was surely even more glad to hear Elizabeth's realisation that this was no ordinary child.

--- **REFLECTION** ---

Heavenly Father, thank you for taking the everyday happenings of friendship and investing them with your miraculous power.

Quietly overturning the world

And Mary said, My soul doth magnify the Lord, And my spirit hath rejoiced in God my Saviour. For he hath regarded the low estate of his handmaiden: for, behold, from henceforth all generations shall call me blessed. For he that is mighty hath done to me great things; and holy is his name. And his mercy is on them that fear him from generation to generation. He hath shewed strength with his arm; he hath scattered the proud in the imagination of their hearts. He hath put down the mighty from their seats, and exalted them of low degree. He hath filled the hungry with good things; and the rich he hath sent empty away.

Following on from the previous reading is Mary's response to Elizabeth—the song we know as the Magnificat, here in a version slightly different from the one familiar from the Book of Common Prayer (which has words such as 'lowliness' for 'low estate'). Mary gives thanks in a way that reveals precisely those qualities for which God chose her: her humility and ability to see God at work in the details, and to link this to a larger picture of God's mercy. Her vision of the kingdom is subversive, as the mighty are put down and the lowly raised up. Revolutionaries of many shades have found here divine sanction for social justice.

The Magnificat prepares us for the way the worldly patterns are overturned: everyday things are exalted by God and used for his highest purposes. Ordinary people like Mary, Joseph and the shepherds find themselves centre stage in a drama on which the salvation of the world depends. The hungry are filled with good things: the spiritually empty people of the world, from the wise men downwards, are given real sustenance.

We know that people are desperate for this food (how many times do we hear of spiritual hunger in discussions of modern beliefs, or responses to public deaths, such as that of Diana, Princess of Wales?). One suggestion that could be drawn from the Magnificat is that the filling of this gap comes about through quiet plugging away 'from generation to generation', responding to God's call in a lowly, local way. Just as God fulfilled his will through a peasant girl from the backwater Roman province of Palestine, so he can use us, too.

Even in fleeting encounters in shops or streets, or at the end of church services, we can try to overturn the worldly order and show our concern for the forgotten or the poor.

PRAYER

God my Saviour, thank you for giving me the chance to join with so many others in celebrating your mercy.

'God in nappies'

And in the sixth month the angel Gabriel was sent from God unto a city of Galilee, named Nazareth, To a virgin espoused to a man whose name was Joseph, of the house of David; and the virgin's name was Mary. And the angel came in unto her, and said, Hail, thou that art highly favoured, the Lord is with thee: blessed art thou among women. And when she saw him, she was troubled at his saying, and cast in her mind what manner of salutation this should be. And the angel said unto her, Fear not, Mary: for thou hast found favour with God. And, behold, thou shalt conceive in thy womb, and bring forth a son, and shalt call his name JESUS. He shall be great, and shall be called the Son of the Highest: and the Lord God shall give unto him the throne of his father David.

Many of our Christmas cards feature the annunciation—the beginning of the story in one sense, though of course it can be traced back much further, beyond even the Old Testament prophecies about it, to the creation of the world. In many paintings of the scene, Gabriel bows to Mary—or, more accurately, to the place where the child is about to be formed inside her. This establishes a clear hierarchy: Jesus rules above the angels, including Gabriel, and all creation.

This leads on to the central paradox of Christmas: the Lord of the universe becomes a mere human being. He is not just pretending to be a man as a brief experiment, passing through the world to sample the delights of humanity, like the Greek gods when they visited the earth. He becomes a defenceless baby, reliant on others to survive. As Neil MacGregor, the former Director of the National Gallery in London, has said when talking about Christmas paintings, this is 'God in nappies'. The more we think about this, the more amazing it seems. 'Annunciation' by John Donne (1572–1631) explores some of the paradoxes. Addressing Mary, it ends famously:

> ... thou art now
> Thy maker's maker, and thy Father's mother;
> Thou hast light in dark; and shutst in little room,
> Immensity cloister'd in thy dear womb.

This is the sort of holy mystery we can only partly hold in our minds. But we can contemplate the beauty of its truth, and thank God.

--- PRAYER ---

King of the universe, thank you for sending us your Son to be one of us.

Prepare for the child at the door

Blessed be the Lord God of Israel; for he hath visited and redeemed his people... That he would grant unto us, that we being delivered out of the hand of our enemies might serve him without fear, In holiness and righteousness before him, all the days of our life. And thou, child, shalt be called the prophet of the Highest: for thou shalt go before the face of the Lord to prepare his ways; To give knowledge of salvation unto his people by the remission of their sins, Through the tender mercy of our God; whereby the dayspring from on high hath visited us, To give light to them that sit in darkness and in the shadow of death, to guide our feet into the way of peace.

This reading, set by the Churches for Christmas Eve, is the Benedictus, Zechariah's prophecy over his unexpected newborn son, John. This is what the father says as soon as he is able to speak, having been struck dumb for not believing that he and the elderly Elizabeth would have a child (see 1:5–24, 57–66). Zechariah, like Mary in the previous reading, pours out spontaneous praise to God, linking the particular blessing given to him with the long history of God's goodness to his people. Both know that what has happened isn't really about them, but about God and his abundant grace.

Yet they offer more than thankfulness. Both are announcing the new chapter in God's dealings with humankind, so that we 'might serve him without fear' (v. 74). We have plenty of fears to be saved from. It is like one of the 'Three Poems of Incarnation' (1952) by Kathleen Raine, in which a child is pictured standing at the door 'in darkness and fear', refusing to leave, despite the sin inside the house:

I will not go back for hate or sin,
I will not go back for sorrow or pain,
For my true love mourns within
On the threshold of night.

The child is 'One who waits till you call him in / From the empty night'. We know that Jesus stands at the door and knocks (Revelation 3:20). We can picture the painting by Holman Hunt (one version of which is in St Paul's Cathedral in London), showing him with a lantern outside the door. Now we need to prepare ourselves to let him in.

REFLECTION

Try to spend a few minutes thinking about which of your fears and sins prevent you from getting ready to welcome the Lord.

'Let every heart prepare him room'

And all went to be taxed, every one into his own city. And Joseph also went up from Galilee, out of the city of Nazareth, into Judaea, unto the city of David, which is called Bethlehem; (because he was of the house and lineage of David:) To be taxed with Mary his espoused wife, being great with child. And so it was, that, while they were there, the days were accomplished that she should be delivered. And she brought forth her firstborn son, and wrapped him in swaddling clothes, and laid him in a manger; because there was no room for them in the inn.

———————

After all the weeks of build-up, the nativity happens in a quiet, low-key way. We have to bring our own background knowledge to realise the significance of the event. All births are miraculous and wonderful, but this is more than a happy human event. It's not just Jesus' birthday that we celebrate: it's the salvation of the whole world.

So we go back to the paradoxes of the reading from Luke 1:26–32: the fragile baby being the king of the universe. As the 18th-century poet Christopher Smart wrote:

O the magnitude of meekness!
Worth from worth immortal sprung;
O the strength of infant weakness,
If eternal is so young!

Again, it's hard for our minds and senses to take in so much joy, so much astonishing love. We can only wonder at it. Yet the human and divine blessings are woven together in a way so that everyone can grasp something of it, even if only a small part. The simple happiness of life is knitted with a mystery of grace that not even the super-intelligent can fully fathom. As Smart goes on:

God all-bounteous, all-creative,
Whom no ills from good dissuade,
Is incarnate, and a native
Of the very world he made.

In this world, we can let Jesus 'be born in us today'.

——————— **REFLECTION** ———————

Joy to the world! The Lord is come; let earth receive her King.
Let every heart prepare him room, and heaven and nature sing.

Isaac Watts (1719)

The gifts of ordinary people

And there were in the same country shepherds abiding in the field, keeping watch over their flock by night. And, lo, the angel of the Lord came upon them, and the glory of the Lord shone round about them: and they were sore afraid. And the angel said unto them, Fear not: for, behold, I bring you good tidings of great joy, which shall be to all people. For unto you is born this day in the city of David a Saviour, which is Christ the Lord.

If you look at the nativity scenes on Christmas cards, you'll see how often artists painted the shepherds as ordinary working people of their own day in their scruffy labouring clothes. It's only long after the paintings have become Old Masters that they seem quaint. Even the job of looking after sheep seems prettified to our urbanised society (although, of course, it's extremely hard work being a shepherd—as I know, coming from a long line of shepherds, though our family has swapped relentless, uncertain toil for the comforts of regular hours in warm offices). But the original ordinariness of the shepherds emphasises how God comes to us as we are. The kingdom of God is among us—here and now—not somewhere holy, unreachable or with smart people.

Many poems and plays, especially medieval ones, speak of the shepherds offering presents. Again, this can seem very quaint, as the charming (if sometimes raucous) group give their lowly bits and pieces. In one anonymous medieval poem, Wat the shepherd offers his working tools:

Jesu, I offer to thee here my pipe,
My kilt, my tarbox, and my scrip;
Home to my fellows now will I skip,
And also look unto my sheep.

But, of course, this is all he has. Unlike so many of us now, he doesn't have more clutter than he knows what to do with. Unlike my own son, the infant Jesus doesn't have more toys than he can play with.

So what could we give? We all know the answer from Christina Rossetti's hymn 'In the bleak mid-winter'. Singing these words about giving our heart might give us a warm glow temporarily in a cold church, but perhaps our giving could be more substantial, extending to more of our time, money and talents. How grateful are we for all this joy?

--- **REFLECTION** ---

Is our satisfied and overfull state today a time to resolve to give away
more of what we have?

The darkness did not overcome it

In the beginning was the Word, and the Word was with God, and the
Word was God. The same was in the beginning with God. All things
were made by him; and without him was not any thing made that was
made. In him was life; and the life was the light of men. And the light
shineth in darkness; and the darkness comprehended it not.

In the Church's calendar, several saints—Stephen the first martyr on 26
December and John the Evangelist, author of the Fourth Gospel, on 27
December, for example—are tucked away in the period between Christmas
and New Year. It has become an odd time for many of us, associated more
with turkey leftovers and sale-shopping than saints.

Yet it's appropriate to celebrate John straight after Christmas Day because
of the emphasis in his Gospel on light. This is the same light shining out of
darkness that we saw in the previous reading. Rembrandt's *Adoration of the
Shepherds* in the National Gallery in London shows the nativity happening
in a Dutch barn, in the dark, among a huddle of working people sheltering
against the cold. God comes to them as they are; as his name suggests:
Emmanuel, 'God with us'. His light shines out of the dark night.

In this picture, and still more in others (such as *The Nativity* by Geertgen
tot Sint Jans, also in the National Gallery), the infant Christ himself seems
to be the source of light. Illumination radiates from his very skin, lighting
up Mary and the worshipping angels.

As we have seen throughout the nativity story, everyone can approach
this holy mystery and grasp something of it: everyone can understand the
symbolism of the light shining in the darkness. It speaks of our hopes for
the good and also our fears about the surrounding darkness, which can
seem so powerful. It draws out the loneliness we can all feel (perhaps
especially at such a social time), when we seem on the brink of being
overwhelmed.

But the message goes beyond hope: 'the darkness comprehended it not'
(or 'did not overcome it') (v. 5). Goodness and truth are there, present
within us all, if only we will strive to foster them.

REFLECTION

*'But as many as received him, to them gave he power to become the sons of
God, even to them that believe on his name' (John 1:12).*

The child born to die for us

Then Herod, when he saw that he was mocked of the wise men, was exceeding wroth, and sent forth, and slew all the children that were in Bethlehem, and in all the coasts thereof, from two years old and under, according to the time which he had diligently inquired of the wise men. Then was fulfilled that which was spoken by Jeremy the prophet, saying, In Rama was there a voice heard, lamentation, and weeping, and great mourning, Rachel weeping for her children, and would not be comforted, because they are not.

This is the darkest episode of Christmas: the Massacre of the Innocents. It's a tale of savagery that would seem to sit uncomfortably with the rest of the story. It seems to belong more to the horrors of the modern era: Herod has more in common with ruthless and insecure tyrants such as Hitler, Stalin and Pol Pot than the received notions of the season of goodwill.

But this is the other side of Christmas: the child is born to die for us. In many medieval lyrics, poets imagine lullabies to comfort the infant Jesus' crying. The baby cries because that is what babies do, but this is more, as we saw in the introduction to this section: this is Jesus mourning for the sins of the world, for which he offers himself.

Lullay, for woe, thou little thing,
Thou little bairn, thou little king;
Mankind is cause of thy mourning,
*   That thou hast loved so yore.*
(Note: 'yore' means 'long since')

I have seen the Massacre of the Innocents acted out in medieval mystery plays. Sometimes, it's almost too painful to watch, as the killers go about their business so gleefully and the mothers try to fight back.

Of course, this raises the big question: why didn't God intervene to prevent such sinfulness? Herod chooses to murder innocent children, and no one stops him. He perverts the free will that God has given him. In the prophecy of Jeremiah ('Jeremy' in KJV) quoted here, Rachel is surely right not to be comforted: there can be no easy answer to such searing pain, tearing the babies from their mothers' loving arms to slaughter them.

Sometimes it seems like flimsy consolation, but we can point to God's presence with them in their agony; his support as he suffers with them. He, too, will know what it is like to watch a son die.

--- **REFLECTION** ---

Father, help us to bring your comfort to those who are in need.

Recovering the perspective of heaven

And fear not them which kill the body, but are not able to kill the soul: but rather fear him which is able to destroy both soul and body in hell. Are not two sparrows sold for a farthing? and one of them shall not fall on the ground without your Father. But the very hairs of your head are all numbered. Fear ye not therefore, ye are of more value than many sparrows. Whosoever therefore shall confess me before men, him will I confess also before my Father which is in heaven. But whosoever shall deny me before men, him will I also deny before my Father which is in heaven.

The day after we commemorate the Massacre of the Innocents comes the date when we remember Thomas Becket, 29 December, for he was murdered on that day in 1170. As with the previous reading, we are plunged into the darker side of Christmas. But this is not so bleak: Becket was an astute politician who knew the risks he was running. He could have got away from danger, but instead he chose to witness to his faith.

Much of T.S. Eliot's play *Murder in the Cathedral* (1935) tackles Becket's struggle with the idea of martyrdom. Eliot sees all too clearly the dangers of spiritual pride and of seeking a violent, dramatic death for the wrong reasons. Towards the end of the play, as his killers approach, Becket gains a true sense of the perspective of heaven: 'And I am not in danger: only near to death,' he says. This is an outworking of Jesus' words here in verse 28.

In the sermon that Eliot imagines Becket preaching on Christmas Day, four days before his death, he speaks of the two sides of Christmas that we noted in the Massacre of the Innocents—celebrating Christ's birth at the same time as his death. Becket comments, 'For who in the world will both mourn and rejoice at once and for the same reason?'

This is all part of God's way, and, as we know, God's ways are not our ways. A quick look at our fellow Christians will reassure us of that: we would be unlikely to choose such an odd bunch of people. God has purposes for us all, despite our peculiarities. Martyrs are one extreme example of this. As Becket says in the play, 'The true martyr is he who has become the instrument of God, who has lost his will in the will of God, and who no longer desires anything for himself.'

--- **REFLECTION** ---

What would my life be like if I sensed the perspective of heaven freshly each day?

Sorrow touched with joy

And above all these things put on charity, which is the bond of perfectness. And let the peace of God rule in your hearts, to the which also ye are called in one body; and be ye thankful. Let the word of Christ dwell in you richly in all wisdom; teaching and admonishing one another in psalms and hymns and spiritual songs, singing with grace in your hearts to the Lord. And whatsoever ye do in word or deed, do all in the name of the Lord Jesus, giving thanks to God and the Father by him.

This passage is set for churches to read during the Christmas season, which continues until Candlemas on 2 February. It spells out some of the consequences of Jesus' being born in our hearts: the overflowing of thankfulness to God in a joyful attitude to everything and everyone we meet. 'Charity, the bond of perfectness' (v. 14) can also be translated as something like 'love, which binds everything together in completeness'.

In theory, it should be easy to cultivate this love in the time following on from Christmas Day, when we are brim-full with good food, surrounded by good company, and while the 'psalms and hymns and spiritual songs' are fresh in our minds. We should be inspired by the vision set before us here. Yet, somehow, it doesn't always seem to work out like that, in spite of the number of blessings we could count. Quite apart from the potential for family rows, often we're more conscious of those who are absent at Christmas, rather than being glad of those who are present.

Perhaps we imagine some happier Christmas past, and think of the faces that are missing around the table at dinner. It can be hard to remember to thank God for what our beloved missing ones brought, and to carry on doing everything in Jesus' name (v. 17). But we could try. Tennyson speaks of this in *In Memoriam*. He describes the 'sorrow touched with joy' of the first Christmas after the death of his friend:

With such compelling cause to grieve
As daily vexes household peace,
And chains regret to his decease,
How dare we keep our Christmas-eve?

--- **REFLECTION** ---

Even in the depths of grief, Tennyson makes the effort to turn to God:

> *Rise, happy morn, rise, holy morn,*
> *Draw forth the cheerful day from night:*
> *O Father, touch the east, and light*
> *The light that shone when Hope was born.*

Living in the light of grace and truth

And the Word was made flesh, and dwelt among us, (and we beheld his glory, the glory as of the only begotten of the Father,) full of grace and truth... And of his fulness have all we received, and grace for grace. For the law was given by Moses, but grace and truth came by Jesus Christ. No man hath seen God at any time; the only begotten Son, which is in the bosom of the Father, he hath declared him.

Another of the readings set for this season picks up shortly after the earlier one from John 1:1–5. It contains many of the themes we have been considering: the paradox of almighty God becoming a humble part of his own creation; the outpouring of God's grace; and the combination in Jesus of basic human appeal and divine providence.

Like the passage from Colossians 3, these are inspiring words, which we can struggle to live up to. We are given 'grace for grace' or 'grace upon grace'. It seems hard to connect these blessings to the rough-and-tumble of our everyday world—meeting people, working, shopping, looking after others and being looked after ourselves. But verse 17 points to a way: our lives aren't about fulfilling a set of rules, ticking off a list of qualities and feeling smug about them. For we have a broader and perhaps more difficult aim—to live in the light of God's grace and truth.

The KJV translation of verse 18 is close to the Greek, but modern versions spell it out in a different way—'It is God the only Son, who is close to the Father's heart, who has made him known' (NRSV)—though the KJV is (as so often) more concrete and immediate, with its 'in the bosom of the Father' and 'declared him'. Of course, the good news of Christmas is that we have a human model, a person we can relate to, rather than a set of bare instructions. As Hebrews 1:1–2 (a reading set for Christmas Day) says, 'God, who at sundry times and in divers manners spake in time past unto the fathers by the prophets, Hath in these last days spoken unto us by his Son.' This is the gift that lasts, while so many others are broken or linger unused.

REFLECTION

Let others look for pearl and gold,
Tissues or tabbies [silks] manifold;
One only lock of that sweet hay
Whereon the blessed Baby lay,
Or one poor swaddling-clout, shall be
The richest New-Year's gift to me.

Robert Herrick, 'The New-Year's Gift' (1648)

The Sermon on the Mount

Chapters 5 to 7 of Matthew's Gospel are the heart of Jesus' teaching, containing some of his best-known words, including the Beatitudes and the Lord's Prayer, yet they remain mysterious, even odd. 'Blessed are they that mourn,' he says, for example, and 'If thy right eye offend thee, pluck it out.' Throughout the collection of sayings, he is building up a picture of the values of God's kingdom, which are usually the opposite of what the world thinks important.

Anyone looking for simple rules will be disappointed. Instead, Jesus is telling us about a relationship that we can have with God. He sets out his approach and inspires us to catch the vision. Yes, it is demanding, but God is here with us. He makes it easier for us by giving us ideas about how to pray—most notably the Lord's Prayer.

Jesus' speech here is not like that in laws or instructions. It is exaggerated and poetic. It encourages us to think for ourselves and seek the kingdom of God in any situation. It's a particular Jewish style of speaking, which is important to appreciate for its own qualities, rather than dismissing it for not being like 21st-century common sense. In some places, the extreme nature of Jesus' speech can give us what seems to be an excuse for an over-clever reading, as if we're trying to twist his words to fit with our prejudices. However, we do need to think beyond the plain meaning of, for instance, the idea of cutting off parts of our body if they prevent us from entering the kingdom (5:29–30).

In keeping with this literary approach, the Sermon on the Mount forms a carefully crafted unit within the Gospel as a whole. Matthew hasn't just piled up all the sayings in a random heap but has structured them neatly, often using groups of three. The Lord's Prayer is exactly in the middle of these three chapters.

In contrast with modern translations, the King James Version's more poetic, allusive language suits the way Jesus is talking about something beyond our immediate grasp. The kingdom cannot be reduced so easily to literal-minded terms.

As we can see in the final verse, though (7:29), whatever Jesus said, he said with authority. The people listening to him then were astonished and we are, too. After 2000 years, we're still struggling to fathom these clues to the amazing grace of God.

The world turned upside down

And seeing the multitudes, [Jesus] went up into a mountain: and when he was set, his disciples came unto him: And he opened his mouth, and taught them, saying, Blessed are the poor in spirit: for theirs is the kingdom of heaven. Blessed are they that mourn: for they shall be comforted. Blessed are the meek: for they shall inherit the earth. Blessed are they which do hunger and thirst after righteousness: for they shall be filled.

Matthew opens his collection of some of Jesus' most important teaching with the Beatitudes. Luke's version appears differently: it is shorter and there isn't the same stress on our actions (Luke 6:20–49). Here in Matthew, the first half of each saying describes what life is like now; the second promises hope, which might be fulfilled only in the next world.

The Beatitudes turn this world's values on their head. On one level, they take despised and dreaded things and suggest that good will come from them: 'Blessed are they that mourn: for they shall be comforted' (v. 4). The Beatitudes were the main Gospel reading when one of my friends took his final vows as a monk. The monastic life of renunciation, sharing and obedience represents the reversal of the world's worship of money, sex and personal choice.

This gives the Beatitudes an elusive quality. They are like good poetry—always suggesting further depths of meaning. It's important, too, that they are not commands: 'Blessed are the meek' doesn't mean the same as 'You must be meek.' Instead, they build a picture of the type of people God thinks are special. That is why 'blessed' feels like a better translation than 'happy', as some modern versions have it. Mourners and the poor in spirit aren't happy in any conventional sense, but they can be blessed by God.

God doesn't necessarily want everyone to go around desperately trying to be humble and unassertive: that doesn't work. Rather, Jesus is saying that God values genuinely unassuming people and won't walk all over them in the way that people often do in the world.

So these first four Beatitudes don't mean that we have to try to make ourselves poor in spirit, mourners or meek (though hungering after righteousness could be helpful). Rather, we should be aware that God cherishes people like this. When we get the chance, we can try to value these qualities in others and cultivate them in ourselves.

PRAYER

Father, help me to learn true meekness.

Perhaps the pushy aren't so blessed

Blessed are the merciful: for they shall obtain mercy. Blessed are the pure in heart: for they shall see God. Blessed are the peacemakers: for they shall be called the children of God. Blessed are they which are persecuted for righteousness' sake: for theirs is the kingdom of heaven. Blessed are ye, when men shall revile you, and persecute you, and shall say all manner of evil against you falsely, for my sake. Rejoice, and be exceeding glad: for great is your reward in heaven: for so persecuted they the prophets which were before you.

People have sometimes tried to convey the revolutionary qualities of the Beatitudes by imagining a worldly version as a contrast: 'Blessed are the rich: they will buy everything they want' and 'Blessed are the pushy: they will get their own way.' The strange thing is that we all know secretly in our hearts that only God's values can satisfy our deepest needs, and that worldly values are hollow. Money can't buy us love and not many people really want to be pushing all the time.

So we know that it is actually better to be merciful, because we all need mercy sometimes; and to be pure in heart, because we all struggle with such mixed motives; and to be peacemakers, because drawing up battle-lines isn't the way of love or contentment.

The last two Beatitudes—outlining blessings on those persecuted for righteousness and for the Lord's sake—are even harder to fathom. As we saw in the previous reading, it's not a case of looking to be persecuted, but instead of reminding ourselves of the ultimate values—what really matters.

All this adds up to a picture of the people ignored and even despised by the world, but whom God cherishes. We can glimpse this sometimes in communities, such as the monastery that my friend was joining (see the previous reading), the L'Arche community, where learning-disabled people live alongside others, and those churches where everyone is valued and personal holiness is matched by active concern for others. Many people saw this quality in the six Melanesian Brothers in the Solomon Islands who, in 2003, went unarmed to help another Brother who had been kidnapped. There was no guile in them but they were murdered for their faith. Their sacrifice opened the way for people to see the violence on the islands in a new way, and to look more wholeheartedly for peace.

--- REFLECTION ---

What small action can I do today to reflect God's kingdom?

Glowing with God's grace

Ye are the salt of the earth: but if the salt have lost his savour, wherewith shall it be salted? It is thenceforth good for nothing, but to be cast out, and to be trodden under foot of men. Ye are the light of the world. A city that is set on an hill cannot be hid. Neither do men light a candle, and put it under a bushel, but on a candlestick; and it giveth light unto all that are in the house. Let your light so shine before men, that they may see your good works, and glorify your Father which is in heaven.

If we put the Beatitudes into practice, we become the salt of the earth. We don't accept the world's values, so we stand out and give a distinctiveness to the whole. We're like light, which makes a difference to the whole room. We don't have to be flashed about, just put on a candlestick to shine steadily. Even a tiny flame enables people to see in the dark.

We have to tread the fine line between being different from the world (not swallowed up by its values, not losing our savour) and being proper salt and light, which enhances whatever it comes into contact with, not overwhelming it but bringing out the flavour or colour of what is already there. It's not for us to judge the world (that is what only God can do) but to draw out its good side.

Accordingly, our faith shouldn't be focused on ourselves. It's not about self-improvement, to make us deeply wonderful people. Instead, it's about what we can do for others, for all people, whom God loves. Together we can build up a kingdom of people who turn towards God and find their true fulfilment in him.

As the Benedictine monk Hubert van Zeller wrote (*Considerations*, Templegate, 1974), Jesus has invited us to enter into his light: 'He has asked us not merely to reflect it, but to be it.' This is not glitzy or superficial. Think of your favourite film star: you might describe one of their performances as 'luminous', when they truly inhabit a part and seem to glow with its truth. Imagine yourself being lit by God's grace like that.

Just a grain or two of salt can add a certain extra something. We can each make a difference, however small.

--- **REFLECTION** ---

What have I ever done to enhance others' lives?

With God all things are possible

Think not that I am come to destroy the law, or the prophets: I am not come to destroy, but to fulfil. For verily I say unto you, Till heaven and earth pass, one jot or one tittle shall in no wise pass from the law, till all be fulfilled... For I say unto you, That except your righteousness shall exceed the righteousness of the scribes and Pharisees, ye shall in no case enter into the kingdom of heaven.

This is a vital piece of teaching, which corrects some dangerous misunderstandings that have persisted into the 21st century. Jesus hasn't come to reject the Jewish law. When some Christians imply that the law can be ignored, as if we're above all that now, they are going against Jesus' specific instructions. Paradoxically, their very concern with the law and response to it reveals how much they are still bound by rules rather than thinking about what lies behind them, as Jesus does.

What Jesus is actually saying is that God's kingdom is so completely different from our earthbound ideas that we can barely imagine it. The fulfilment of his law goes beyond all this and does so in extraordinary ways, but does not cancel it out.

Jesus is the fulfilment of the law in himself, so he would hardly then trivialise it. As a good and observant Jew, he cared about it and would never want to see it scorned. Yet he doesn't just say that we should obey the law, but that we should outdo even its great teachers in following it. We've got to be even keener than the most devout people. As we saw with the Beatitudes, God's ways are so far from our ways that we can only hope to catch something of his vision to inspire us. His ways are ideals set before us, not strictures of impossible perfection that we can only fail to achieve as we attempt to carry them out.

So Jesus exaggerates. When he wants to tell us that no one can do this by human effort, he surely means that we must realise all the more why we need God. We ought to sense how dependent we are.

REFLECTION

'Who then can be saved?' ... 'With men, this is impossible; but with God all things are possible' (Matthew 19:25–26).

God's ways are not our ways

Ye have heard that it was said by them of old time, Thou shalt not kill; and whosoever shall kill shall be in danger of the judgment: But I say unto you, That whosoever is angry with his brother without a cause shall be in danger of the judgment: and whosoever shall say to his brother, Raca, shall be in danger of the council: but whosoever shall say, Thou fool, shall be in danger of hell fire. Therefore if thou bring thy gift to the altar, and there rememberest that thy brother hath ought against thee; Leave there thy gift before the altar, and go thy way; first be reconciled to thy brother, and then come and offer thy gift.

Jesus continues his exaggeration of exactly how righteous we should be. One of the curious things about it is the mixture of extreme idealism and common-sense wisdom. Some of it seems so down-to-earth that no one could disagree with it, but other parts seem so heavenly minded as to be no earthly use.

Are we really not supposed to get angry? Shouldn't we be angry at cruelty and suffering, or angry as Jesus himself was with the abuses of the money changers in the temple, and as God was in the Old Testament over Israel's sins? Surely this is all part of Jesus' pushing things to extremes to show how completely we need to immerse ourselves in God's ways and just how different they are from ours. We need to lose our box-ticking approach to good and bad, as if we have a checklist of sins. This so often has an edge of 'I'm better than you.' Instead, we should embrace a larger vision of God's whole kingdom.

Such an approach might mean that, in the end, we do great good things, but it has to start first with the attitudes behind these views and actions. So we need to look at what leads us into sins such as murder and examine the anger in our own hearts. Then we can see that there is not such a great dividing line between law-abiding religious people and thieves, murderers and rapists. We are all human and all need God's mercy.

REFLECTION

'For my thoughts are not your thoughts, neither are your ways my ways, saith the Lord' (Isaiah 55:8).

Note: 'Raca' in verse 22 is translated elsewhere as 'insult' (NRSV) or 'a term of contempt' (NIV footnote).

A call to wholeness

Ye have heard that it was said by them of old time, Thou shalt not commit adultery: But I say unto you, That whosoever looketh on a woman to lust after her hath committed adultery with her already in his heart. And if thy right eye offend thee, pluck it out, and cast it from thee: for it is profitable for thee that one of thy members should perish, and not that thy whole body should be cast into hell. And if thy right hand offend thee, cut it off, and cast it from thee: for it is profitable for thee that one of thy members should perish, and not that thy whole body should be cast into hell.

The wild exaggeration continues. Have you ever heard of Christians mutilating themselves like this? If the Archbishop of Canterbury preached such a sermon today, he might be carried off for psychological investigation.

Clearly, Jesus is talking about ideals, not concrete realities. One way to look at this might be to compare the way he is going beyond mere keeping of the rules to what is called virtue ethics, which emphasises the importance of basic character rather than simply what people do or say. This approach encourages people to develop virtues such as, here, respect for others—not seeing them as objects for personal gratification (sexual or otherwise)—and self-control and discernment about personal sins.

Virtue ethics can be discussed in a purely secular way, but it has parallels with Jesus' vision of the kingdom. He is calling us to be people of integrity.

This passage isn't saying that it is wrong to have lustful thoughts, but that it is wrong to savour them and let them lead us into sin. The Greek words (here translated 'to lust after her') have a sense of moving towards something. It's something we should try to turn our backs on, and move away from.

These words also suggest how much the kingdom should matter to us. We know that it's not supposed to be just a delightful hobby or even a way of life that makes us feel fulfilled, although we often seem to behave as if that is all it is. Instead, Jesus says it's like a pearl of great price, in that it means so much to us that we will dispense with everything else we have in order to keep the kingdom alone (Matthew 13:46).

REFLECTION

Is there anything that stops me from following Jesus wholeheartedly? What about money, the way I think of others, and my desire for an easy life?

Beyond plain speaking to integrity

It hath been said, Whosoever shall put away his wife, let him give her a writing of divorcement: But I say unto you, That whosoever shall put away his wife, saving for the cause of fornication, causeth her to commit adultery: and whosoever shall marry her that is divorced committeth adultery. Again, ye have heard that it hath been said by them of old time, Thou shalt not forswear thyself, but shalt perform unto the Lord thine oaths: But I say unto you, Swear not at all... But let your communication be, Yea, yea; Nay, nay: for whatsoever is more than these cometh of evil.

In contrast to the earlier parts of the Sermon on the Mount, these would seem like straightforward instructions. So why do many, if not most, Christians go against these clear commands from our Lord? How can we possibly justify divorce on the grounds of, for example, violence? How can we defend swearing on the Bible in court?

Jesus seems to be pointing towards what Paul later described as the contrast between the spirit and the letter of the law (2 Corinthians 3:6). He knows that divorce is definitely not a matter of a simple certificate. It is a devastating ripping apart of one flesh—like a death. Our Western society, however, has gone to the other extreme and tries to pretend that it is not a great problem.

Clearly whole books could be (and have been) written about this, so what follows are only suggestions, in the context of the Sermon on the Mount as a whole. These chapters paint a picture of a wider approach as to how we ought to behave—broader than just looking at particular rules. They seem to be saying that we should cultivate healthy attitudes and the values of the kingdom in every way we can. We should search for God's values, not our natural selfish wishes: 'seek ye first the kingdom of God' (Matthew 6:33). If we try to see situations as God sees them, we will surely be merciful to others and generous concerning their problems, rather than taking it on ourselves to judge them.

MEDITATION

Pray for those in troubled and broken relationships. Think of at least one thing you might do to support them.

Dare to surrender your goods

Ye have heard that it hath been said, An eye for an eye, and a tooth for a tooth: But I say unto you, That ye resist not evil: but whosoever shall smite thee on thy right cheek, turn to him the other also. And if any man will sue thee at the law, and take away thy coat, let him have thy cloak also. And whosoever shall compel thee to go a mile, go with him twain. Give to him that asketh thee, and from him that would borrow of thee turn not thou away.

The theologian Jane Williams suggests that Jesus tells us here to be 'foolishly generous to others', even to allow ourselves 'to be treated unfairly by the greedy and the powerful and the anxious because we know that nothing they can do can actually dispossess us' (*Lectionary Reflections*, SPCK, 2004).

Some of the people who are most at home in the kingdom are like this. While certainly not meek and mild, they have the type of fearlessness that doesn't mind about more blows landing on their other cheek. They sit so lightly to their own comfort and long-term security that they freely give away their belongings. (St Richard of Chichester seems to have been like this: see the readings focusing on him in the penultimate section of this book.) Would I have anything like the guts to do that? I don't think so.

All the same, these words give me a vivid image of the sort of person I should try to be. I shouldn't think myself generous just because I give to others from my loose change and spare possessions, but I should donate sacrificially, sharing my most treasured blessings.

It's hard to think of anyone who is so free from the all-encompassing snare of worldly goods that they ever behave like this. Perhaps another friend in the religious life, a Franciscan friar, comes closest. He certainly has more freedom, having given up his 'right to choose'. He has relinquished the objects that the rest of us hug to ourselves as a comfort blanket—the gratification that comes from choosing our own clothes, work, companions and possessions. Sometimes it seems as if these things are all that we have to define ourselves, but thinking in this way means that we are missing out. If only we would dare to surrender them, we might find that there are other, greater blessings.

Of course, there is one person who lived this philosophy perfectly: Jesus himself. In his suffering and death, he turned the other cheek and didn't demand his rights.

PRAYER

Father, help me to realise that my true security lies with you.

The perfect approach to good and bad

But I say unto you, Love your enemies, bless them that curse you, do good to them that hate you, and pray for them which despitefully use you, and persecute you; That ye may be the children of your Father which is in heaven: for he maketh his sun to rise on the evil and on the good, and sendeth rain on the just and on the unjust. For if ye love them which love you, what reward have ye? do not even the publicans the same? ... Be ye therefore perfect, even as your Father which is in heaven is perfect.

How much further can Jesus push this? He has already sketched the most special people in the kingdom as being the despised, persecuted and dispossessed. Now he sums it up by saying, 'Be perfect.' That's all? Should be a doddle...

Of course, we know that we can never be perfect, but that doesn't mean we should give up. A healthy attitude could be summarised as a case of both 'If a thing's worth doing, it's worth doing well' and also 'If a thing's worth doing, it's worth doing badly.' We need to keep trying afresh every morning. Being 'perfect' doesn't mean being sinless, either. The Greek word is *teleios*, which is more like 'finished', 'whole' or 'having integrity'.

The big point is that we're not doing this on our own. Jesus calls us to be perfect like our heavenly Father ('even as your Father', v. 48). We're in a relationship with a loving parent who can help us. This is a Father who sends sun and rain on good and bad alike. That is what we have to try, too—loving dodgy people as well as nice ones, and not expecting anything back. If we truly have the Spirit of Jesus within us, we'll find ourselves doing this as a matter of course, not because it's sensible or practical (it isn't either of those things, but it is the way of love).

Some Christians wouldn't approve of this: they'd call for a boycott on sinners. Certainly God isn't having much regard for purity here, but what he is saying is that the impulse to draw boundaries and to grade who's in and who's out of God's love isn't religious at all. It's just another way of the world—a grubby human desire to bolster ourselves up as the in-crowd by picking on other people as the unclean crowd.

--- **REFLECTION** ---

If God sends rain on the just and the unjust, can we ever judge who might fall into either category?

Depending on God

Take heed that ye do not your alms before men, to be seen of them: otherwise ye have no reward of your Father which is in heaven. Therefore when thou doest thine alms, do not sound a trumpet before thee, as the hypocrites do in the synagogues and in the streets, that they may have glory of men. Verily I say unto you, They have their reward. But when thou doest alms, let not thy left hand know what thy right hand doeth: That thine alms may be in secret: and thy Father which seeth in secret himself shall reward thee openly.

Matthew groups together various religious activities—almsgiving and, in the verses after this passage, prayer and fasting—not just to recommend them but to outline how they should be carried out. He stresses that all these activities should be done in secret.

This is about more than just avoiding showing off (though spiritual pride worms its way into the most intimate places of our hearts). It is about not doing the right thing for the wrong reason. If we're being religious in outward ways for the sake of the reward of heaven and praise from others, what does that make us? Nasty little creeps, always looking away from the matter in hand to check on what other people think, and thinking that we can fool God.

This is a long way from the wholehearted love we were asked to have for people in the previous reading. It's easy to fall into the trap of keeping our faith and what is really important to us in separate compartments. We can so easily choose to be religious in one tiny way and limit our faith to particular choices, and then act as if we don't depend on God.

The fact is that we do depend on God for everything, and almsgiving, along with prayer and fasting, should remind us of that. It should also remind us that we're part of the wider world that God loves. He cherishes the poor and the hungry, who don't have much choice about fasting and have little to give away. We're all in this together and all equally loved by God. How can we fail to help and love the people God loves?

PRAYER

Father of us all, fill every corner of my being so that I overflow with your love and generosity.

Your Father knows you

And when thou prayest, thou shalt not be as the hypocrites are: for they love to pray standing in the synagogues and in the corners of the streets, that they may be seen of men. Verily I say unto you, They have their reward. But thou, when thou prayest, enter into thy closet, and when thou hast shut thy door, pray to thy Father which is in secret; and thy Father which seeth in secret shall reward thee openly. But when ye pray, use not vain repetitions, as the heathen do: for they think that they shall be heard for their much speaking. Be not ye therefore like unto them: for your Father knoweth what things ye have need of, before ye ask him.

As we saw in the previous reading, it's all too easy to think of faults such as hypocrisy belonging to someone else—perhaps a pompous person at church or, historically, particular groups of first-century people. These words, though, are directed squarely at us now.

Have you ever caught yourself lingering in prayer, wanting to appear spiritual? Even in private (and 'closet' here just means 'private room'), have you ever piled up many good causes or elegant phrases, pleased with your own fluency or the number of people you're praying for? God knows what we want, regardless of how we present our pleas; perhaps he smiles at our pretensions. We should present ourselves to him without any dissembling. Yet again, Jesus stresses that it is our underlying approach that is important, not how we seem or what we actually do as we pray.

We have all tried to pray in empty phrases ('vain repetitions' and 'much speaking'—which seems much sharper than 'their many words' in modern translations). It is demonstrated in the old story of the person who explained that they pray simply by sitting in church quietly alone: 'I look at God, and he looks at me.' I've met people who assume that individual prayer is always like this and are surprised that the story comes as a revelation to others, who had got bogged down in elaborate wording.

Often, however, we need something—perhaps words, the way we sit or kneel, a picture, icon or candle—to ease us into that state where we become aware of God's power and love. The United States President Theodore Roosevelt used to take his guests outside to see the stars after grand diplomatic dinners. He would gaze up and remind them how vast the distances were in space. Then he would end, 'Do we feel small enough now?'

--- REFLECTION ---

What helps you to become aware of God's presence?

Beneath God's overarching love

After this manner therefore pray ye: Our Father which art in heaven, Hallowed be thy name. Thy kingdom come, Thy will be done in earth, as it is in heaven. Give us this day our daily bread. And forgive us our debts, as we forgive our debtors. And lead us not into temptation, but deliver us from evil: For thine is the kingdom, and the power, and the glory, for ever. Amen. For if ye forgive men their trespasses, your heavenly Father will also forgive you: But if ye forgive not men their trespasses, neither will your Father forgive your trespasses.

At last, after the teaching about general approaches to prayer, Jesus gives us some actual words. But, of course, they don't tell us everything. As we've heard before, we need to be wholehearted about them, praying them from deep inside with our whole being.

It's useful to read the Lord's Prayer as part of the Sermon on the Mount, seeing how it puts into practice the themes of the Beatitudes and other teachings. It begins with 'Our Father', stressing the family relationship between each one of us and our loving Creator. This is where all our yearning springs from, both between people and for God. This is where our prayer and fasting and giving have their source.

Yet this loving Father is also the holy one, far above the sins of the world. He is our hope for life in heaven in the future, though he is intimately bound up with us now. This hallowedness is what should make us realise that the meek and those who grieve for the state of the world are correct. Being poor in spirit before almighty God is only right. We should pray that the kingdom—the world of the Beatitudes and selfless giving—is brought about. In this kingdom, we have our needs but they are part of the pool of others' needs. It's a reciprocal situation. We forgive others and they forgive us, all under the loving rule of God. We can only pray for his overarching love to protect us from the judgment to come, as we acknowledge our debt to and dependence on him. We are sinners, each and every one of us, and we need to approach others, our fellow offenders, with the same attitude of mercy that we hope for ourselves rather than presuming to judge them.

PRAYER

Pray this version of the Lord's Prayer, lingering over each phrase and thinking how it applies to your situation today.

Where is your treasure?

Lay not up for yourselves treasures upon earth, where moth and rust doth corrupt, and where thieves break through and steal: But lay up for yourselves treasures in heaven, where neither moth nor rust doth corrupt, and where thieves do not break through nor steal: For where your treasure is, there will your heart be also... No man can serve two masters: for either he will hate the one, and love the other; or else he will hold to the one, and despise the other. Ye cannot serve God and mammon.

Only last week, I found that my beautiful favourite cardigan had some holes where a moth had got at it. Thankfully, it's mendable, but finding it in that state made me unduly upset, not least because it was partly my fault. I have some lovely clothes—more than I need—but am I grateful to God for such luxury every time I get dressed? Not really. Could I give them away tomorrow to those who need them more than I do? Not without a terrible but ultimately ridiculous feeling of loss.

I read about someone who had all his possessions stolen. They had been packed in a removal van and he had only the clothes he stood up in. He was devastated, but family and friends rallied round and gave him things and cash to buy more. When he began to acquire new goods, though, he felt he'd lost something—some of the freedom of not possessing anything.

Most of us store up treasures, whether clothes, household goods or a pension fund, but it's the underlying attitude to them that matters. Could we manage without them? When we get a sense of how much we rely on such things, even love them, we glimpse how much we can and should depend on God. We can see how our whole self is wrapped up in these possessions when, really, to be healthy and true, it ought to be wrapped up in God.

REFLECTION

My words and thoughts do both express this notion,
That Life hath with the sun a double motion.
 The first Is straight and our diurnal friend,
  The other Hid and doth obliquely bend.
One life is wrapped In flesh, and tends to earth.
The other winds towards Him, whose happy birth
   Taught me to live here so That still one eye
Should aim and shoot at that which Is on high:
     Quitting with daily labour all My pleasure,
      To gain at harvest an eternal Treasure.

George Herbert (1633)

Knowing we're part of God's kingdom

Take no thought for your life, what ye shall eat, or what ye shall drink;
nor yet for your body, what ye shall put on. Is not the life more than
meat, and the body than raiment? … Consider the lilies of the field,
how they grow; they toil not, neither do they spin: And yet I say unto
you, that even Solomon in all his glory was not arrayed like one of
these… your heavenly Father knoweth that ye have need of all these
things. But seek ye first the kingdom of God, and his righteousness;
and all these things shall be added unto you.

Jesus develops the theme of the previous reading in this rightly celebrated
passage. Reading it within the Sermon on the Mount, we can see that
he is emphatically not judging the many people who have died for lack of
food and clothing. As Jane Williams puts it, 'Are we to assume that they
somehow failed to concentrate sufficiently on the kingdom, and so were
punished…? I think not.'

Instead, Jesus is urging us to focus on what is really important and turn
away from our anxieties. Yes, there are economic interests that are keen to
keep us buying stuff that we don't need, but surely the real problem is our
selfish hearts. We don't recognise what will be truly satisfying and, instead,
palm ourselves off with inferior junk, whether it's food, possessions or feel-
good experiences. We cling on to things that can't ever meet our needs.
We're like children who want to eat only sweets: no wonder we become
sick at heart.

What can we do to realign ourselves with what God has designed to
fulfil us? Jesus says simply that our priority should be the kingdom of God
and God's righteousness. It sounds straightforward enough, but, of course,
it's not that easy. We so easily wander away in our thoughts and can't manage from our own reserves of strength, but at least we can start each day
by setting it within the framework of God's care for us and his kingdom.

REFLECTION

*As you begin the day, try to imagine what you're going to do in a fresh light.
Seek God in your actions, the people you're going to meet
and your reactions to events.*

There is no competition

Judge not, that ye be not judged… why beholdest thou the mote that is in thy brother's eye, but considerest not the beam that is in thine own eye? Or how wilt thou say to thy brother, Let me pull out the mote out of thine eye; and, behold, a beam is in thine own eye? Thou hypocrite, first cast out the beam out of thine own eye; and then shalt thou see clearly to cast out the mote out of thy brother's eye.

This is a good reading for a Sunday. Isn't each one of us guilty of judging our fellow Christians in church, in however small a way? This is just what the world sees—Christians as hypocrites, nitpicking at others when we, too, are flawed. Jesus utterly rejects this human failing and tells us firmly to sort ourselves out. As in the parable of the workers in the vineyard (Matthew 20:1–16), we shouldn't be looking over our shoulders at what others are doing, but making a sustained search of our own hearts.

Like other passages throughout the Sermon on the Mount, this one seems to be about cultivating a particular habit of mind, with God's help. It's much more than just trying to be nice, like a decent person; it's about our whole way of being, as Jesus also suggested in his image of getting all our nourishment from him: 'I am the vine, ye are the branches' (John 15:5).

Prayer must be at the heart of this. There has to be a personal meeting with God and time spent being in his love. When we know that we are in the presence of God, we find it harder to judge others. When we have some inkling of God's love and his sacrifice for us, his sheer goodness gives us a hint of our own sinfulness. God has given so much to me, and to each of my brothers and sisters, that my responses seem pathetic in comparison. There should be no other kinds of comparing, though. We are each bathed in his light, so that silly distinctions between my wickedness and my brother's or sister's are exposed as meaningless in God's glorious kingdom of love.

REFLECTION

Think about how much God has done for you and how flimsy your judgments of others seem in that light.

Given good things by your Father

Ask, and it shall be given you; seek, and ye shall find; knock, and it shall be opened unto you: For every one that asketh receiveth; and he that seeketh findeth; and to him that knocketh it shall be opened... If ye then, being evil, know how to give good gifts unto your children, how much more shall your Father which is in heaven give good things to them that ask him? Therefore all things whatsoever ye would that men should do to you, do ye even so to them: for this is the law and the prophets.

As we move towards the end of the Sermon on the Mount, the mood winds down with reassurances and summing up. It seems to suggest that if all these habits of perfection seem too far out of reach, we should try asking God about the whole business. While this sounds crushingly obvious, it still feels hard to do. God longs to welcome us back to bask in his love, so why do we behave like spoilt children who don't know how blessed they are? Why don't we come close to him? What are we afraid of?

Perhaps we are anxious that God doesn't really love us after all. Some of us just don't realise when we're loved and find it hard to believe that anyone could care for us. Sometimes there's a slow process of realising that God has given everything for us and wants to give us even more. Also, other people share God's love for us, too.

More often, though, we can't believe that God will give us what we're asking for, so we mistakenly feel that there's no point in even trying to bring our needs to him. Perhaps we should let God be the judge of that and approach him honestly with all our desires. He can sort through the self-serving wishes and twisted motives, giving us what we really need.

--- **REFLECTION** ---

King of glory, King of peace,
I will love thee...
Thou hast granted my request,
Thou hast heard me...
Wherefore with my utmost art
I will sing thee,
And the cream of all my heart
I will bring thee.
Though my sins against me cried,
Thou didst clear me;
And alone, when they replied,
Thou didst hear me.

George Herbert (1633)

The right way to call on the Lord

Enter ye in at the strait gate: for wide is the gate, and broad is the way, that leadeth to destruction, and many there be which go in thereat: Because strait is the gate, and narrow is the way, which leadeth unto life, and few there be that find it... Wherefore by their fruits ye shall know them. Not every one that saith unto me, Lord, Lord, shall enter into the kingdom of heaven; but he that doeth the will of my Father which is in heaven.

The warnings here are terrifying. Suddenly, it's personal. It's about nice people like us who faithfully read our spiritual books. If I'm the one saying 'Lord, Lord...', is Jesus knocking down my attempt at being a decent Christian, while also saying that there will be few who manage it? I'm tempted to agree with Teresa of Avila when she became so angry with God that she exclaimed, 'Look at how you treat those who love you', as if to say, 'No wonder you have so few friends.'

Scholars, however, tell us that Jesus is deliberately exaggerating, as he did when talking about cutting off limbs (Matthew 5:28–30). As before, it's the underlying attitude he is getting at—a defensive self-righteousness. Those of us who think we're in with the boss are in the most danger. We can fall into some serious misconceptions, such as thinking that we've become righteous by our own efforts and, fatally, that we're better than others. As in the parable of the Pharisee and the tax collector (Luke 18:9–14), it's the self-confessed sinner who goes away justified, not the upright, overtly religious one: 'How blessed are those who know their need of God' (Matthew 5:3, NEB).

The Sermon on the Mount is coming full circle, leading us back to the Beatitudes' picture of the whole approach we should live out before God. Following Jesus isn't about doing outwardly religious deeds but about loving and becoming like him. We still shout, 'Lord, Lord' like petulant children who have wandered away from God, though we expect him still to be at our beck and call. We need to be transformed from within.

PRAYER

Father, keep me in your love, so that my ways become your ways.

Building on the rock of love

Therefore whosoever heareth these sayings of mine, and doeth them, I will liken him unto a wise man, which built his house upon a rock: And the rain descended, and the floods came, and the winds blew, and beat upon that house; and it fell not... And every one that heareth these sayings of mine, and doeth them not, shall be likened unto a foolish man, which built his house upon the sand: And the rain descended... and great was the fall of it... When Jesus had ended these sayings, the people were astonished at his doctrine: For he taught them as one having authority, and not as the scribes.

The Sermon on the Mount ends with an image of itself—as a solid foundation that we can build on. If we follow the approach that Jesus outlines, we'll be able to cope with all sorts of storms. It's like the love between couples or in families: if we have this kind of strong bond, we can cope with whatever the world throws at us.

It has also been suggested that the storms mentioned are those of the end times. We need to build our lives on the rock of God's righteousness in order to stay firm when his judgment comes.

So how can we summarise 'these sayings'? They seem to be about realising our place in the world, within God's overarching care. Everything falls into place. It's not our world, but God's, so we should look after it. Everything we have comes from God, so we should be grateful to him; otherwise we're deceiving ourselves about the true state of the universe. God is greater and far more loving than us selfish humans, so let's not become overly proud of any 'achievements'. It's a case of our facing up to this reality, not fending God off as we so often do.

Once we have a sense of the way in which God cares for us, we'll be people who are secure enough not to need to show off to get anyone's approval of our faith—people who love even our enemies, and are the salt of the earth.

PRAYER

Pray the Lord's Prayer again in the light of the values shining out from the Sermon on the Mount—love, trust in God, self-forgetfulness and concern for others.

Holy Week

These eight readings cover Jesus' journey from the adulation of Palm Sunday, on through his teaching in the temple, to Maundy Thursday and the last supper, before the agony in the garden of Gethsemane, then his betrayal, arrest and trials. We then see his crucifixion, death and burial and, finally, Easter Day. It's daunting to stand on the brink of these events, but so it should be: these are matters of life and death for us all.

For most of these readings, we are using the passages set by the ecumenical Revised Common Lectionary, which is read in many churches (and is largely the same as the *Common Worship* lectionary used in Anglican churches). They are taken from the Gospel of Luke—a Gentile writing for the fledgling Christian communities in about AD80–85.

Luke's writing has much in common with Matthew's and Mark's and, together, their works make up the three 'synoptic' Gospels. These three have similar views on Jesus' life, whereas John comes at it from a different angle. Luke still has a distinctive voice, however, standing out even from Matthew and Mark in, for instance, stressing Jesus' faith in his heavenly Father at the crucifixion rather than a sense of abandonment. Luke also seems more concerned for those on the fringes, such as the women who are present at Jesus' burial and his resurrection, than he is with the crucifixion itself.

The passages are familiar to most of us: we've heard them many, many times and heard many sermons about them. We therefore think we know exactly what is going to happen, so we need to look for ways to make them breathe again. Using the KJV is especially helpful in addressing this issue. Many of us know the translation but might not have heard it read out in church recently. Paradoxically, the old words can draw us to the events being described in a fresh way. They can jolt us into re-examining what is happening, and pondering on its significance. The language here also seems more vivid. For example, 'But he perceived their craftiness' (Luke 20:23) seems more lively and profound than 'He saw through their duplicity' (NIV) or 'Jesus knew that they were trying to trick him' (GNB).

More importantly, though, whatever words we use, the truths we are looking at are unaltered: Jesus lived, died and rose again for us.

Every stone shall cry

The whole multitude of the disciples began to rejoice and praise God with a loud voice for all the mighty works that they had seen; Saying, Blessed be the King that cometh in the name of the Lord: peace in heaven, and glory in the highest. And some of the Pharisees from among the multitude said unto him, Master, rebuke thy disciples. And he answered and said unto them, I tell you that, if these should hold their peace, the stones would immediately cry out.

———————

Luke's presentation of Jesus' entry into Jerusalem—the event we celebrate as Palm Sunday—isn't as triumphal as it is in the other Gospels. Matthew, Mark and John have a larger crowd, drawn from many in Jerusalem, who acclaim Jesus. Here, though, only the disciples rejoice. The Pharisees' response confirms this, as they refer only to 'thy disciples', as if Jesus' immediate followers are responding on behalf of all the people. It's like when people ask Christians to pray for them ('Say one for me') and to do what they themselves can't or won't do: go and seek God.

There is a sense here in which someone or something cannot suppress acclamation of Jesus. If the disciples didn't praise him, the seemingly cold stones would have had to speak out. If people cannot fulfil their creaturely destiny and express the praise they were made to give, other parts of creation would have had to do it for them. Rejoicing in God is a gut response that we can hardly stop ourselves doing for our loving Father. To deny it makes us less than human and closes our hearts to love.

When people ask 'Say one for me', they are probably, without knowing it, acknowledging that turning to God is something we all need to do. It's not a case of dull duty but a natural urge that we should admit the source of our life and hope. If we don't do this, if our hearts are harder than rock, the stones themselves will step in to acclaim our Saviour. The poet Richard Wilbur (b. 1921) expressed this when he wrote:

And every stone shall cry
For stony hearts of men:
God's blood upon the spearhead,
God's love refused again.

———— **REFLECTION** ————

Where can you openly acknowledge God's work today?

How separate is the world from God?

And they asked him, saying, Master… Is it lawful for us to give tribute unto Caesar, or no? But he perceived their craftiness, and said unto them, Why tempt ye me? Shew me a penny. Whose image and superscription hath it? They answered and said, Caesar's. And he said unto them, Render therefore unto Caesar the things which be Caesar's, and unto God the things which be God's.

Now that he is in Jerusalem, the spies sent by the chief priests and scribes try to trap Jesus with an impossible question. Of course, there is no right answer and, whatever he says, he will be open to criticism. As usual with Jesus, though, he takes on board their words and moves the conversation to a different level.

The words 'Render unto Caesar…' have inspired a huge range of responses. Some use the phrase as an excuse for being completely otherworldly, fulfilling their obligations to society in the most minimal way and ignoring the needs of fellow humans. Others go to the opposite extreme and see it as justification for immersing themselves in worldly business, keeping a little corner of their souls for God but not letting it intrude on the rest of their lives.

I don't believe that the phrase means there is to be a complete separation between God and the world, as if he isn't bothered about his creation. We know from his great love for us, and his sending his Son, that he is profoundly involved in it.

Among other lessons that this rich teaching gives us is a hint of the temptation for many of us to assume that there is a 'Christian view', a party line, on every detail of our lives. Don't get me wrong, the hairs of our heads are numbered and God cares passionately about us, but not everything is a test of faith. Alan Bennett, in his *Talking Heads* (BBC, 1988) television monologue 'Bed among the Lentils', refers (only half-jokingly) to a trendy vicar attending 'the usual interdenominational conference on the role of the Church in a hitherto uncolonised department of life, underfloor central heating possibly'. There are many aspects of our lives that we simply need to get on with, in a faithful spirit, rather than agonising about where they stand in the whole created order.

REFLECTION

'Love, and be silent.'

Shakespeare, *King Lear*

81

Giving from our abundance

And he looked up, and saw the rich men casting their gifts into the treasury. And he saw also a certain poor widow casting in thither two mites. And he said, Of a truth I say unto you, that this poor widow hath cast in more than they all: For all these have of their abundance cast in unto the offerings of God: but she of her penury hath cast in all the living that she had.

———————————

Jesus, teaching in the temple in Jerusalem, points out to his listeners some of the other visitors. He contrasts those who donate 'of their abundance'—out of their wealth, with plenty still in their pockets—with the widow who gives from her poverty, 'all the living that she had'. The Greek word here for 'living' (or 'livelihood', *bios*) is the same as the word for life itself, so there is a sense, too, in which she gives her life.

This tells us that giving isn't about the numerical total of what has been donated but about the character of the giver—their approach to what they have and what they have left after giving. It's about people, not things.

At the Lambeth Conference (the gathering of Anglican bishops from all over the world that takes place every ten years) in 2008, there were people from the richest, most expensively equipped churches, worshipping and studying the Bible with those from the poorest places on earth, who had few buildings or books. How could the two extremes relate to each other?

I put this question to Jane Williams, wife of the Archbishop of Canterbury, who was organising the programme for the bishops' wives and husbands. She said that one of the main things was just getting to know one another, getting to feel what was important to the other person and how they experienced God and the world. She knew this couldn't solve all the problems, but it was a way in. 'People begin to trust each other's good faith,' she said. 'Even if it reaches conclusions you don't agree with, you know the other people are trying to be disciples.'

——————— **REFLECTION** ———————

Can we put a face to our giving, and give out of our abundance to those who have little? Does your church have links with people and places in need of the basics, while we have more than we really need?

Becoming Jesus' body

And he took the cup, and gave thanks, and said, Take this, and divide it among yourselves: For I say unto you, I will not drink of the fruit of the vine, until the kingdom of God shall come. And he took bread, and gave thanks, and brake it, and gave unto them, saying, This is my body which is given for you: this do in remembrance of me. Likewise also the cup after supper, saying, This cup is the new testament in my blood, which is shed for you.

We are looking ahead here to the events that we mark on Maundy Thursday, when churches celebrate Jesus' founding of the Lord's Supper, the Holy Communion or Eucharist. It's a small moment of joy amid the atmosphere of suffering and death—modified rapture, perhaps.

Among other things, Jesus is reminding us here of why this is happening. He is doing this for us, on our behalf—but, of course, it's much more than that. He is giving us something that we can carry out to remember him and to join with him in one of the most intimate ways we can imagine. By sharing his body, we can be part of him, here and now. Millions of us across the world are brought together in this way, built up into a mighty body. We can be the hands and feet of Jesus, as the 16th-century mystic Teresa of Avila noted: 'Christ has no Body now but yours, no hands, no feet on earth but yours.'

The Communion service, in whatever Christian tradition we encounter it, works on so many different levels at the same time. Sometimes, in church, the words and actions seem impossibly rich and bewildering, while at other times they seem beautifully simple. We can become one with Jesus. We can be strengthened, fed by the nourishment of Jesus' very self, sacrificed once for us. This is something solid, which we can feel and touch. As John Chrysostom said, writing in the fourth century: 'Our Lord hands over to you, in tangible things, that which is perceived by the mind.'

-------- REFLECTION --------

He was the Word that spake it,
He took the Bread and brake it,
And what that word did make it,
That I believe, and take it.

Queen Elizabeth I (1533–1603)

Turning from evil to good

[Jesus] said unto [the disciples], Pray that ye enter not into tempta-tion. And he was withdrawn from them about a stone's cast, and kneeled down, and prayed, Saying, Father, if thou be willing, remove this cup from me: nevertheless not my will, but thine, be done. And there appeared an angel unto him from heaven, strengthening him. And being in an agony he prayed more earnestly: and his sweat was as it were great drops of blood falling down to the ground.

———————

Gethsemane speaks to each of us directly about those moments when we think something like, 'If only I didn't have to go through this. Please, God, take it away.' Maybe it is a medical operation, childbirth, an interview, a difficult meeting or some other seemingly impossible trial. Even if there is no way out of enduring the terror, as there was no escape for Jesus, there are crumbs of comfort in both God's presence with us and the knowledge that Jesus has been here, too, and can empathise with us: 'in all points tempted like as we are' (Hebrews 4:15).

Sometimes, though, this just doesn't seem enough, and we really can't cope. It is then that we have to throw ourselves on God, pray hard, and look for the support of other people. Often, it is not the one-off crisis or decision that brings us to breaking-point, but the relentless dull ache of having to keep going—perhaps because of illness, lack of money, fraught relation-ships or intractable people. At such times we have to try, if only feebly, one step at a time, to turn to the good wherever we can.

It reminds me of a part in *Persuasion* by Jane Austen, where the heroine visits an old schoolfriend who, despite having a serious illness that limits what she can do, still manages to be positive and even generous to others:

A submissive spirit might be patient, a strong understanding would supply resolution, but here was something more; here was that elasticity of mind, that disposition to be comforted, that power of turning readily from evil to good, and of finding employment which carried her out of herself... It was the choicest gift of Heaven.

——————— PRAYER ———————

Heavenly Father, help me to turn to you in times of trouble.
Carry me through the pain.

Reaching out to us in love

And it was about the sixth hour, and there was a darkness over all the earth until the ninth hour. And the sun was darkened, and the veil of the temple was rent in the midst. And when Jesus had cried with a loud voice, he said, Father, into thy hands I commend my spirit: and having said thus, he gave up the ghost. Now when the centurion saw what was done, he glorified God, saying, Certainly this was a righteous man.

Luke's treatment of the crucifixion is not as bleak as Mark's or Matthew's (the two other Gospels that are closest to his). Jesus does not cry out in desolation that his Father has forsaken him. Instead, he prays for his tormentors—'Father, forgive them...' (23:34) and reassures the penitent thief: 'Today shalt thou be with me in Paradise' (v. 43).

Luke focuses on Jesus' resignation, which here is almost serenity, as he gives himself to his Father, using the words of Psalm 31:5 ('Into thine hand I commit my spirit'). He accepts his torture quietly. This is a confident surrender, firm in the hope accompanying it. The world might not understand, but his action is the opposite of cowardice or being a doormat. It is a realistic facing up to suffering and a refusal to retaliate: even if he was outnumbered and pinned down so that he couldn't have fought back, he could have exchanged violent words, but he chose not to.

This is very much the same Jesus whom Luke has presented throughout his Gospel. His true nature shines through. He is welcoming to the penitent thief, as he had been welcoming to other outsiders, such as women, tax collectors and various sinners. This means that there is less emphasis on the cross as an isolated phenomenon and more on it as a continuation and culmination of Jesus' life. It's his whole life, as well as his death, that is our pattern and inspiration.

Jesus has done nothing but good and here he is paying the ultimate price as if he were evil. He stretches out to us in love and we—or our representatives, at any rate—kick him in the face.

REFLECTION

His gracious hands, ne'er stretched but to do good,
Are nailed to the infamous wood:
And sinful Man does fondly bind
The arms, which he extends t'embrace all human kind.

Abraham Cowley, 'Christ's Passion' (1663)

Waiting between death and hope

And all the people that came together to that sight, beholding the things which were done, smote their breasts, and returned. And all his acquaintance, and the women that followed him from Galilee, stood afar off, beholding these things. And, behold, there was a man named Joseph, a counsellor; and he was a good man... This man went unto Pilate, and begged the body of Jesus. And he took it down, and wrapped it in linen, and laid it in a sepulchre... And the women... returned, and prepared spices and ointments; and rested the sabbath day according to the commandment.

This feels like the tidying up of loose ends. As with so many tasks after a death, there is an overwhelming feeling of going through the practicalities, perhaps being grateful to have something to get on with, in order to avoid the well of emptiness that Jesus' death has created.

The disciples were in that bleak state of waiting around but not expecting anything to happen. The fact that we know what is going to happen next shouldn't stop us from pausing here and waiting with them. There is a strange and sometimes awkward pause on the evening of Good Friday and through Holy Saturday.

This is a special time, which can give us a sense of being between two worlds. There is the world of sin, suffering and death, where retaliation, casual violence and thoughtless cruelty are routine. There is also before us, in the distance, the world of almost unimaginable hope. Here now, though, there is only the waiting. It is like a miniature version of our life, waiting for the second coming. As W.H. Auden says in his play *For the Time Being* (1944), we live 'between the times' of Jesus' coming to earth and his coming again.

In this state, we can only turn to God in the sure and certain hope of the resurrection. It might seem incredible now, in the middle of grief, but it will come.

REFLECTION

Be near me when my light is low,
When the blood creeps, and the nerves prick
And tingle; and the heart is sick,
And all the wheels of Being slow.

Alfred, Lord Tennyson, *In Memoriam*

Miracles can happen

Now upon the first day of the week, very early in the morning, they came unto the sepulchre, bringing the spices which they had prepared... And they found the stone rolled away from the sepulchre. And they entered in, and found not the body of the Lord Jesus. And it came to pass, as they were much perplexed thereabout, behold, two men stood by them in shining garments: And as they were afraid, and bowed down their faces to the earth, they said unto them, Why seek ye the living among the dead? He is not here, but is risen.

In Luke, the resurrection seems particularly mysterious. The women visit the tomb to anoint Jesus' body, and it is clear from these and later verses that they have precious little clue about what is happening. It will take a great miracle to turn them away from the ever-deepening furrows of their grief at Jesus' death and towards the amazing, undreamt-of future, for which they have no pattern and no expectation. But miracles do happen.

The resurrection happened. Jesus rose from the dead and is risen. Other kinds of resurrections can happen today, too, in the world and in our own lives. Many doubted that apartheid would end in South Africa or that the Iron Curtain would fall or that a mixed-race man could become president of the United States, but these things happened. Some of us don't really believe that positive change can come about for us personally. Perhaps we don't think that we'll ever be able to cope with illness or hardship or without one special person. There seems to be no hope and we would rather stay among the dead than seek the living or the living God; but God can draw goodness out of the bleakest situation. He has done it before and will do so again.

Archbishop William Temple summed up the importance of resurrection, as distinct from immortality:

The method of all non-Christian systems is to see an escape from the evils and misery of life. Christianity seeks no escape, but accepts these at their worst, and makes them the material of its triumphant joy. That is the special significance in this connection of the Cross and Resurrection of Jesus Christ.
From *Nature, Man and God* (Macmillan, 1934)

PRAISE

Alleluia, he is risen!

The meaning of the cross

For these 14 readings on the theme of the cross, we are looking not so much at the events of Good Friday as at its wider significance. This can be done not just in Lent but at other times, too, such as in September, as 14 September is Holy Cross Day, an ancient festival when Christians traditionally remember the cross and its place in their lives. Lutherans use the day for special preaching about the theology of the cross, Roman Catholics call the festival the Triumph of the Cross, and Eastern Orthodox Christians call it the Exaltation of the Cross.

It marks the day when the Church of the Holy Sepulchre in Jerusalem was dedicated in AD335. There is a legend that St Helena, the mother of Constantine (who became the Roman Emperor in 306 and later became a Christian like his mother), discovered the cross on which Jesus died in Jerusalem. She is said to have founded the Church of the Holy Sepulchre soon afterwards, on the site of Jesus' burial. It became a place of pilgrimage, which it has continued to be over the centuries.

During Lent and Easter, we usually focus on what happened in and around Jerusalem at that time, but there can be a danger of skipping over what the cross means. One of the key points is that we should never see the cross on its own: it must always be seen in the light of the resurrection. As Cally Hammond says in her Lent book, *Passionate Christianity* (SPCK, 2007):

The first Christians... saw everything to do with Jesus in the light of the resurrection. Their faith, their understanding, their desire to reach out to others, were all conditioned by the absolute, overwhelming conviction that 'God has made him both Lord and Messiah, this Jesus whom you crucified' (Acts 2:36)... They saw a simple, clear connection between the fact of the resurrection and Jesus' acceptance of death as—somehow—necessary and right.

Most of the first half of the Bible readings are those set by churches, including the Anglican and Roman Catholic Churches, to be read on Holy Cross Day, while the second half's passages explore the meaning of the cross, as it was being worked out by Paul and the early Church.

Redeeming an instrument of torture

And they bring him unto the place Golgotha, which is, being interpreted, The place of a skull. And they gave him to drink wine mingled with myrrh: but he received it not. And when they had crucified him, they parted his garments, casting lots upon them, what every man should take. And it was the third hour, and they crucified him. And the superscription of his accusation was written over, THE KING OF THE JEWS.

We begin the readings about the cross at the place where it all started: Jesus being crucified. Before we think about everything that the cross means and does for us, it is important to start with the most obvious facts. The cross was the instrument of an extremely painful and shameful death, deliberately used by the Roman forces of occupation to oppress their subject people in the harshest and most humiliating way they could devise. On the surface, it would be hard to see any good coming out of the cross: it looks like pure defeat.

At various times, Christians have emphasised the horrific torture Jesus suffered. We can see this in gory medieval paintings and carvings, which must have rung true for people in ages when life was nasty, brutish and short. We have had a more recent reminder of this tradition in Mel Gibson's surprisingly popular film, *The Passion of the Christ* (2004). It used the stomach-churning techniques of horror movies to impress on the audience the pain that Jesus endured.

All this seems a long way from celebrating the cross as a symbol. It might appear strange to use an instrument of torture and murder as a sign on our buildings and as a piece of jewellery. We wouldn't think of doing the same thing with a hangman's noose. Strangely, of course, it is only because of the terrible suffering that took place on it—and, most importantly, what happened later—that we can make the cross a light to illuminate our lives; it is only because of Jesus' death and resurrection that the cross is at the centre of our faith now.

 **PRAYER**

Father of all, thank you for the cross on which your Son, our Saviour, died. Help us to absorb its power and meaning into the fabric of everything we do and say and are.

— NUMBERS 21:5–8 (ABRIDGED) —

Trapped in restless ingratitude

And the people spake against God, and against Moses, Wherefore
have ye brought us up out of Egypt to die in the wilderness? …
And the Lord sent fiery serpents among the people, and they bit the
people; and much people of Israel died. Therefore the people came
to Moses, and said, We have sinned, for we have spoken against the
Lord, and against thee; pray unto the Lord, that he take away the serpents from us. And Moses prayed for the people. And the Lord said
unto Moses, Make thee a fiery serpent, and set it upon a pole: and
it shall come to pass, that every one that is bitten, when he looketh
upon it, shall live.

This incident is from the wanderings of the people of Israel in the desert,
after they had left Egypt. It has traditionally been seen as a forerunner
of the cross: the image of something malign and dangerous is transformed
into something that heals; what used to lead to death now gives life. Today,
the serpent entwined on a pole is a symbol of the medical profession.

God seems to be reminding the people of their utter dependence on
him. They complain and are severely punished. Then they repent and are
healed (though many have already died). It seems so simple. If only we
would trust God more and realise what was best for us, everything would
go well. But we don't. We nurse our own warped sense of what we think
is right. We cling on to our petty ideas of self. It's as if we trap ourselves
in an ungenerous, ungrateful attitude to our Father in heaven, who made
us to love him.

Often, although we are reluctant to admit it, we cherish God's creations
instead of the Creator himself. The poet George Herbert describes God as
saying that humankind 'would adore my gifts instead of me'. So, Herbert
continues, God gives us the restlessness that should lead us back to him,
which is the only place where we can find true rest.

--- REFLECTION ---

Let him be rich and weary, that at least,
If goodness lead him not, yet weariness
May toss him to my breast.

George Herbert, 'The Pulley' (1633)

All for love

And no man hath ascended up to heaven, but he that came down from heaven, even the Son of man which is in heaven. And as Moses lifted up the serpent in the wilderness, even so must the Son of man be lifted up: That whosoever believeth in him should not perish, but have eternal life. For God so loved the world, that he gave his only begotten Son, that whosoever believeth in him should not perish, but have everlasting life. For God sent not his Son into the world to condemn the world; but that the world through him might be saved.

This is the Gospel passage that a number of churches set for Holy Cross Day, 14 September. As noted in the Introduction on page 88, this isn't so much about the events of Good Friday as about what the cross does for us in the widest sense. So the word 'cross' is not mentioned, but we find one of the most celebrated verses in the Bible, John 3:16: 'For God so loved the world…'

This is all about looking to God—like looking to the serpent in the previous reading—realising our dependence on him, as the Israelites had to in the wilderness, and trusting him to heal us. If we do this, we will live.

God does not want to condemn us but to save us (v. 17). He has always loved us and his greatest wish is that we might love him and our fellow creatures. It is this love that the cross represents so powerfully. In another part of the poem quoted below, we are told that this love brought Jesus from heaven: 'For love thou hung on rood tree' ('rood' being an old word for 'cross'). It is not just a question of feeling sorry for Jesus' suffering, but of our responding to the love he is pouring out for each one of us.

This is demanding love, 'costing not less than everything', as T.S. Eliot put it in *Little Gidding* (1942). Jesus and his Father suffered grievously to bring us this love and forgiveness. How do we react?

--------- **REFLECTION AND PRAYER** ---------

Jesu, thy love be all my thought,
Of other thing ne reck me nought;
Then have I thy will all wrought,
That havest me full dear bought.

Anonymous medieval lyric
(Note: 'reck' means 'care for')

The humble and meek exalted

Ye that fear the Lord, praise him... For he hath not despised nor
abhorred the affliction of the afflicted; neither hath he hid his face
from him; but when he cried unto him, he heard... The meek shall
eat and be satisfied: they shall praise the Lord that seek him: your
heart shall live for ever. All the ends of the world shall remember and
turn unto the Lord.

This part of Psalm 22 is also set by the churches for Holy Cross Day, to be
read before the Gospel passage we had in the previous reading. There is
a long Christian tradition of seeing this psalm as reflecting the crucifixion—
particularly because of phrases such as 'why hast thou forsaken me?' (v. 1)
and 'they pierced my hands and my feet' (v. 16)—and it is used in church
on Maundy Thursday. (I have written more about this in the section on the
Psalms at the beginning of this book.)

Yet the passage we have here is taken from later in the psalm and it
speaks of God's meeting the needs of the poor. In some ways, it seems an
odd choice for churches to use, but it does forge a link with the familiar
New Testament idea of Jesus coming to rescue humankind by being born
as one of us. We shall follow through this theme in the next passage, which
is from Philippians.

It might seem a long way from the cross, but it is, in fact, the reason
for Jesus' journey from heaven to that place of pain. He came because he
loves his people, especially the poor, and he cares about their 'affliction' (v.
24). The Magnificat echoes this, drawing on God's concern for the lowly
throughout the Old Testament: 'He hath put down the mighty from their
seats, and exalted them of low degree' (Luke 1:52).

So here is the cross as the culmination of one of the central themes of
the Old Testament—God's burning desire to bring justice and honour to
those who are despised by the world. He achieves this by becoming one of
those lowly, rejected people, reaching to the ultimate limit of dying as an
abused criminal.

--- **REFLECTION** ---

*How can I make more links between God's love for us all and the
suffering of the poor? What am I doing today to join in God's care
for those whom most of us ignore?*

Laying aside our selves for others

Let nothing be done through strife or vainglory; but in lowliness of mind let each esteem other better than themselves. Look not every man on his own things, but every man also on the things of others. Let this mind be in you, which was also in Christ Jesus: Who, being in the form of God, thought it not robbery to be equal with God: But made himself of no reputation, and took upon him the form of a servant, and was made in the likeness of men: And being found in fashion as a man, he humbled himself, and became obedient unto death, even the death of the cross.

This reading takes up the theme from the previous passage, in that it fills in the detail of what was needed in order to save the world and bring justice for the poor. Jesus had to empty himself—to strip himself of all his capabilities and status as the second person in the Trinity to become an ordinary man. He was to be stripped further by the Roman soldiers to become the lowest of despised men.

This takes us to the heart of what the cross is about. It shows Jesus letting go of the power, the sense of security and the knowledge of being valued—everything that the people of the world most crave—and undergoing the worst that that world can throw at him. It reminds us how far he had to go in order to bring us home.

Jesus decides to lay aside his life and abilities, so as to give us life. The 17th-century poet Richard Crashaw teases this out in his poem, 'Christ Crucified', where he describes Jesus bound on the cross, his hands nailed down but still willing and able to choose freely to give himself for us:

Thy hands to give thou canst not lift,
Yet will thy hand still giving be;
It gives, but O, itself's the gift!
It gives though bound, though bound 'tis free!

REFLECTION

Is there something I need to do this week to leave behind the comforts that cocoon me from the wants of others and to reach out to them? Is there something more I can give to share the same love as Christ?

The painful path to glory

Wherefore God also hath highly exalted him, and given him a name which is above every name: That at the name of Jesus every knee should bow, of things in heaven, and things in earth, and things under the earth; And that every tongue should confess that Jesus Christ is Lord, to the glory of God the Father.

These famous verses follow straight on from the previous passage and form the contrast between Jesus' death on the cross and his being exalted by God in glory. We are invited to exult in the cross of Christ—to turn the shameful instrument of death into something wonderful that we can celebrate. How on earth can we do this?

Perhaps one clue is in the route Jesus took, which the prayer below emphasises. That involves seeing suffering as an essential element on the path to glory. Pain, like death, is unavoidable, but we do have a choice about how we meet it. Obviously we can try not to be embittered by suffering, but our choice concerns whether or not we should expect it in the first place.

Some of us (especially in Western societies) seem surprised by any troubles we meet, as if we had some bizarre right to be treated better than anyone else. We know, deep down, that being a Christian does not protect us from suffering, but we sometimes behave as if we had earned the right to float above it. Earlier generations were more in touch with physical hardship and death in the midst of life than we are today. Because of that, many of them had a stronger sense of their dependence on God. We, in contrast, have more to be thankful for, because of technological and medical advances, but seem to find it harder to be grateful to God than did people in earlier days.

The Collect (the special prayer that collects together themes) for Holy Cross Day (below) brings together pain and exaltation, and weaves them into the wholeness that Christ offers us. On the one hand, there is humiliation, suffering and death; on the other, life, reconciliation with God and glory.

PRAYER

Almighty God, who in the passion of thy blessed Son hast made an instrument of painful death to be for us the means of life and peace: grant us so to glory in the cross of Christ that we may gladly suffer for his sake.

Common Worship

Lose your life, for God's sake

Then said Jesus unto his disciples, If any man will come after me, let him deny himself, and take up his cross, and follow me. For whosoever will save his life shall lose it: and whosoever will lose his life for my sake shall find it. For what is a man profited, if he shall gain the whole world, and lose his own soul? or what shall a man give in exchange for his soul? For the Son of man shall come in the glory of his Father with his angels; and then he shall reward every man according to his works.

The rest of the Bible passages for these readings on the theme of the cross move beyond those set for Holy Cross Day by the churches to look at other ideas associated with it. In the order in which they appear in the New Testament, these passages actually start well before the crucifixion itself. One of the main threads is that of taking up our own cross of self-denial for the sake of Christ.

This develops what we read in the previous verses from Philippians, about suffering and glory being inextricably bound together, and moves it into a different area—that of deliberately choosing to leave behind caring for ourselves in order to follow Jesus. The image is one of our willingly shouldering a burden in order to imitate Christ and draw closer to him. We would gain a sense of focusing so much on him that we forget about our own needs, troubles and desires.

Following on from the reading from Numbers 21, in connection with the Israelites' clinging on to their sinful ways in the wilderness instead of trusting God, this is another way to describe the universal tendency to cherish our own delights. Many of us do something horribly similar. We would rather nurse our selfishness than open ourselves up to love and allow God and other people in: 'Men loved darkness rather than light, because their deeds were evil' (John 3:19).

REFLECTION

We need a wider perspective and an eternal timeframe to help us move away from selfishness towards the love of God:

> *The world's light shines; shine as it will,*
> *The world will love its darkness still:*
> *I doubt though when the world's in hell,*
> *It will not love its darkness half so well.*

Richard Crashaw, 'But Men Loved Darkness rather than Light' (1646)

The cost of discipleship

And there went great multitudes with him: and [Jesus] turned, and said unto them, If any man come to me, and hate not his father, and mother, and wife, and children, and brethren, and sisters, yea, and his own life also, he cannot be my disciple. And whosoever doth not bear his cross, and come after me, cannot be my disciple. For which of you, intending to build a tower, sitteth not down first, and counteth the cost, whether he have sufficient to finish it?

Jesus is saying more than just 'Focus on me and forget yourself.' He is asking us to weigh up whether or not we are prepared for the cost of taking up our cross. He knows that if we do not do this, we will fall away. We need to take our discipleship seriously enough that we do not get swept up in our new enthusiasm, like a passing fad that fades as quickly as it came.

The cross is the ultimate symbol of this. It means that we can die to whatever separates us from God. So we should consider carefully whether or not we are prepared to take up this work of love, which may involve turning away from those closest to us and from life itself (v. 26).

Ought we really to neglect our responsibilities for God's sake, though? Jesus uses deliberately exaggerated language ('hate not...' is a figure of speech for 'loveth... more than me', which is how it is worded in the equivalent passage in Matthew 10:37). Jesus does not suggest abandoning any obligations to them but perhaps means, rather, that we should not rely on them completely for our ultimate happiness. He might well be critical of the modern tendency to idealise family life, weighing it down with the intolerable burden of being the source of our fulfilment. Many of us are guilty of worshipping this idol rather than God.

We need to be wholeheartedly for God, responding to the love shown on the cross with an unstinting love of our own.

--- **REFLECTION** ---

But just the way that thou didst me
I do love and I will love thee:
What must I love thee, Lord, for then?—
For being my king and God. Amen
Gerard Manley Hopkins (1844–89), 'O Deus, Ego Amo Te'

The world doesn't understand

For the preaching of the cross is to them that perish foolishness; but unto us which are saved it is the power of God... For the Jews require a sign, and the Greeks seek after wisdom: But we preach Christ crucified, unto the Jews a stumblingblock, and unto the Greeks foolishness; But unto them which are called, both Jews and Greeks, Christ the power of God, and the wisdom of God. Because the foolishness of God is wiser than men; and the weakness of God is stronger than men.

Despite its being an instrument of oppression and judicial murder, the cross has been transformed into something that demonstrates the power and wisdom of God. No wonder most people don't understand it.

As with the Beatitudes and the rest of the Sermon on the Mount, God turns the wisdom of the world on its head: 'Blessed are they that mourn', 'Love your enemies, bless them that curse you' (Matthew 5:4, 44). It's the opposite of normal common sense (see the section earlier on the Sermon on the Mount for more on this). But then God's wisdom is so utterly different that it gets to the heart of life in a much deeper way. He exposes our foolish wickedness.

God redeems us, buying back what was and really is his own by thoroughly undermining the wrongdoing that can drive a wedge between him and us. Jesus' actions on the cross show us a better way to respond to the wickedness around us. Jesus meets the cruelty of his torturers with kindness. He knows that they do not realise what they are doing. His pure heart beats with the same pulse as his Father's.

God's kingdom is ordered differently from the world, so we need each day to realign ourselves with his values. The world does not understand them and so is the ultimate loser. People abandon their souls as they struggle to reach the top, only to find that their victories are hollow.

--- **PRAYER** ---

Lift up our minds to the pure, bright serene atmosphere of thy presence; that we may breathe freely, there repose in thy love, there be at rest from ourselves and from all things that weary us: and thence return, arrayed in thy peace, to do and to bear whatsoever shall best please thee, O blessed Lord.

E.B. Pusey (1800–82)

Reconciled through the cross

For it pleased the Father that in him should all fulness dwell; And, having made peace through the blood of his cross, by him to reconcile all things unto himself; by him, I say, whether they be things in earth, or things in heaven. And you, that were sometime alienated and enemies in your mind by wicked works, yet now hath he reconciled in the body of his flesh through death, to present you holy and unblameable and unreproveable in his sight.

───────────────

At last, we reach one of the most familiar ideas relating to the cross—that what Jesus did there brought together God and human beings. We, his creatures, had wandered away from our loving creator through sin: the KJV word 'alienated' (v. 21) sums it up neatly, and sounds remarkably modern. But Christ on the cross brought us back home. Most of us know the old drawing of a chasm with God on one side, humankind on the other, and the cross forming a bridge between the two.

Over the centuries, Christians have put forward a number of different ideas about exactly how this works—the theories of the atonement. One of the commonest of these is that Jesus took upon himself the punishment for humans' sins, and died because someone had to pay the price for such wickedness. This is so familiar that many Christians haven't really heard of any other possible approaches, but other Christians see it differently.

They are unhappy about the possible implication that God the Father is so angry about sin that he needs to punish people, including his own Son. They prefer to talk about Jesus' willing sacrifice, bringing us closer to God, in the same way that giving up something for the sake of others can transform a situation.

This approach sees the cross and resurrection as being inextricably linked: that is, Jesus represents us all so that we can join in his death to sin as well as his resurrection. We share in this sacrifice every time we celebrate Holy Communion, recalling his death and rising again.

─────────── **REFLECTION** ───────────

Almighty God, our heavenly Father, who of thy tender mercy didst give thine only Son Jesus Christ to suffer death upon the cross for our redemption; who made there (by his one oblation of himself once offered) a full, perfect, and sufficient sacrifice, oblation, and satisfaction, for the sins of the whole world…
Holy Communion service (Book of Common Prayer)

Nail in the coffin

Buried with him in baptism, wherein also ye are risen with him through the faith of the operation of God, who hath raised him from the dead. And you, being dead in your sins and the uncircumcision of your flesh, hath he quickened together with him, having forgiven you all trespasses; Blotting out the handwriting of ordinances that was against us, which was contrary to us, and took it out of the way, nailing it to his cross.

This is where the language of the KJV sounds complicated at first. It's the type of passage that might make us reach for a modern version. But it takes just one or two words to be explained, and it becomes clearer. For example, the 'handwriting of ordinances' (v. 14) refers to the record of sins.

Whichever way we explain it, Christians know that Christ died for our sins on the cross. One vivid way to express this is Paul's idea here of nailing our sins to the cross. In this way we can put them to death so that they can no longer have power over us. Paul links this to baptism and the crucial Christian idea that some things—good as well as bad—have to die completely before they can be raised to new life. As Jesus himself said, 'Except a corn of wheat fall into the ground and die, it abideth alone: but if it die, it bringeth forth much fruit' (John 12:24: 'abideth alone' could also be translated 'remains just a single grain'). Sin desensitises us, as, when we know we are doing wrong, we suppress our better instincts, which would lead us to a covenant with God (hence 'uncircumcision of your flesh', circumcision being a sign of God's covenant with humankind).

The idea of dumping our unpleasant aspects, nailing them to the cross, is hugely appealing, but what about the parts that we sneakily think are not so bad? There are those talents and attitudes in which we take a self-satisfied pride, fancying ourselves a little better than the next person. Are we ever content to give ourselves over to God and let him decide?

We have to die fully with Christ, not just partially. We cannot hold back those parts of ourselves that we think we can do all right with, thank you. That is surely what the cross means—complete death to the old self (see also Galatians 6:14–15).

PRAYER

I am no longer my own but yours. Put me to what you will, rank me with whom you will; put me to doing, put me to suffering… let me have all things, let me have nothing: I freely and wholeheartedly yield all things to your pleasure and disposal.
From the Methodist Covenant Service

— 1 PETER 2:23–25 —

'Burn off my rusts'

Who, when he was reviled, reviled not again; when he suffered, he
threatened not; but committed himself to him that judgeth righteously: Who his own self bare our sins in his own body on the tree,
that we, being dead to sins, should live unto righteousness: by whose
stripes ye were healed. For ye were as sheep going astray; but are now
returned unto the Shepherd and Bishop of your souls.

This is the next stage in the cosmic significance of the cross. Christ has
taken the initiative and is suffering for us in order to heal us. As we saw
in the previous reading, we need to submit ourselves fully to this process
and join in with his actions. This is part of what we do at Communion services, re-enacting his sacrifice. It is an amazing privilege that we can share
actively in this in our worship.

These steps towards healing can be painful. If we are wholeheartedly
subjecting ourselves to his loving gaze, we should start to see ourselves
as he does—the best as well as the worst. It's always a useful exercise to
try to see situations and our part in them from another person's point of
view—'some Pow'r the giftie gie us / To see oursels as others see us', as
Robert Burns put it. It's even more useful to imagine what God might think
of it all. We are made in his image, so the pattern is there for us to follow.

The thoroughly worthwhile question 'What would Jesus do?' has
become almost a cliché, a motto for bracelets and ballpoint pens. All the
same, it hints at a great truth—that God can guide us through anything
that might be thrown at us. We can 'live unto righteousness' in each circumstance (v. 24). When we are healed and back at home in God, we will
be able to face our troubles in his strength, by his grace.

REFLECTION

O think me worth thine anger, punish me,
Burn off my rusts, and my deformity,
Restore thine image, so much, by thy grace,
That thou may'st know me, and I'll turn my face.
John Donne, 'Good Friday, 1613, Riding Westward'

Raised to life with God

Now if we be dead with Christ, we believe that we shall also live with him: Knowing that Christ being raised from the dead dieth no more; death hath no more dominion over him. For in that he died, he died unto sin once: but in that he liveth, he liveth unto God. Likewise reckon ye also yourselves to be dead indeed unto sin, but alive unto God through Jesus Christ our Lord.

Here the words of the KJV are straightforward: they ring out clearly, once we are used to the old verb endings, such as 'dieth' and 'hath'. This celebrated passage further unpacks the way that the cross has to be seen in the light of the resurrection. Jesus has done his work on the cross, once for all time and all people, so that we can be released from the power of sin and death.

This is why many Christians prefer to display an empty cross. Jesus is no longer there, for he has risen. Other Christians, while fully realising this, want to emphasise that Jesus died on the cross, undergoing that pain for us. They prefer a crucifix showing a figure of Christ suffering, but reaching out to us in love. Both these aspects of his life are true and we need to reflect on both of them at different times.

Whichever way we think about the precise workings of it, we can see that Jesus' sufferings on the cross mean that God knows from the inside the worst of what it is like to be human. It also means that, in his turn, Jesus can raise us from misery, towards his own godliness. As the Collect for the first Sunday of Christmas puts it, 'as he came to share in our humanity, so we may share the life of his divinity' (*Common Worship*).

We are raised with him—not just away from sin and death, but further, towards God. The Orthodox Church has made more of this truth than we have in the West. Irenaeus, a Greek who lived from around AD125 to 202 and was Bishop of Lyons in France, wrote, 'God has become what we are, so that we might become what God is.'

REFLECTION

'As we keep this feast [of the Cross], we are lifted up with the crucified Christ, leaving behind us earth and sin, so that we may gain the things above.'
Andrew of Crete (c. 660–740), a sermon on the exaltation of the holy cross

New every morning is the love

Wherefore seeing we also are compassed about with so great a cloud of witnesses, let us lay aside every weight, and the sin which doth so easily beset us, and let us run with patience the race that is set before us, Looking unto Jesus the author and finisher of our faith; who for the joy that was set before him endured the cross, despising the shame, and is set down at the right hand of the throne of God.

We don't allow ourselves much triumph. It can so easily turn into boasting and, for those of us who are British, it lacks the self-deprecating humour that we like to think is our natural mode. We should triumph in the victory of the cross, though. It was hard-won and that battle was fought specially for us.

An Anglo-Saxon poem offers an approach that can encourage an appropriate sense of triumph. Written anonymously some time between the seventh and tenth centuries, 'The Dream of the Rood' tells of a vision of the cross, now honoured and covered in jewels. It imagines the cross itself speaking about Jesus, seeing him as a triumphant warrior, not a victim—truly 'the author and finisher of our faith' (v. 2): 'The young hero—who was God Almighty—stripped himself, resolute and strong; he mounted the gallows, brave before the crowd: he wished to redeem mankind.'

How can we recover this sense of confidence in our everyday lives? We can approach the truths of our triumphant faith in ways that give it new life. One way that I have found helpful is to do so through poems, such as those that I have quoted in this book. We can also try to be more attentive in our prayer lives to what Jesus did on the cross and our loving response. Could we carve out a little more time to recall this each day?

I have read purely secular magazine articles suggesting that one of the ways to boost inner contentment is to remember gratefully at the end of each day the things that have gone well. Surely we can do better than this pale version of true happiness, starved as it is of the love of God and the warm thankfulness we can feel for our Father and Creator.

--- **REFLECTION** ---

What can I do today to build my confidence in God and help myself realise how amazing divine love is? At the end of the day, list three or more things for which you are now especially grateful.

Jesus after the resurrection

The way that our faith is based on the resurrection can sometimes make us take it for granted. We think about it on Easter Sunday, but perhaps forget that every Sunday is a celebration of it. What is more, the Easter season lasts even longer than Lent: there are 40 days from Easter Sunday to Ascension Day—exactly matching Lent—but Easter continues for an extra ten days, right up to Pentecost (the word 'Pentecost' means '50 days' in Greek).

We have some idea what Lent is about, and many of us manage a little extra effort during those 40 days, whether it takes the form of reading a Lent book, going to a study group or to special church services. So why do we find it comparatively hard to engage with a 50-day season of celebration? You'd think we might be glad of the chance to rejoice.

Partly, I think it has to do with taking God for granted and not pausing to ponder, and rejoice in, what he has done for us.

In the eleven readings that follow, the disciples are stopped in their tracks and forced to see things with new eyes. On the road to Emmaus and when he appears later in the same chapter (Luke 24), Jesus explains the scriptures to the disciples, opening up familiar words in a new way. Both this and, more importantly, the fact that he has risen from the dead are causes of great wonder.

We need to recover that sense of wonder, to stop and be amazed at God's goodness. This can be difficult, as so much of contemporary society runs counter to such thinking, and the media's obsession with bad news and controversy only adds to the problem. Little things can help, though. I remember taking our baby, then aged about six months, to a slightly musty stately home. He was enthralled by the paintings on the walls, gazing at them intently. To the rest of us, they looked rather dull and second-rate— no Rembrandts here, but a load of anonymous portraits of long-forgotten old men. Yet, following his lead, we saw them with fresh eyes, opening ourselves to the wonder of God's gift of creativity.

In a similar way, we need to find ways—even little ways in passing moments—to see the resurrection anew and revel in God's goodness, both during the Easter season and every Sunday.

'My Lord and my God'

But [Thomas] said unto [the disciples], Except I shall see in his hands the print of the nails, and put my finger into the print of the nails, and thrust my hand into his side, I will not believe. And after eight days again his disciples were within, and Thomas with them: then came Jesus, the doors being shut, and stood in the midst, and said, Peace be unto you. Then saith he to Thomas, Reach hither thy finger, and behold my hands; and reach hither thy hand, and thrust it into my side: and be not faithless, but believing. And Thomas answered and said unto him, My Lord and my God.

Doubting Thomas comes across as such a sympathetic figure. Like many of us, he doesn't see why on earth he should give credit to any wild stories of a dead man coming back to life, with his wounds still visible. It all seems like so much wish-fulfilment—perhaps a mass hallucination by a group of frightened people in the throes of grief for their charismatic leader. Indeed, this is how many doubters interpret the New Testament accounts to this day.

Thomas seems like a down-to-earth type, a man who likes to know where he stands and feel things solidly in his hands. There's nothing wrong with this. He could be just the sort of practical person I'd like to come and mend my boiler. This is the same man who, earlier in this Gospel, asked Jesus, 'Lord, we don't know where you are going, so how can we know the way?' To this perfectly sensible question, Jesus gave the inspiring answer, 'I am the way and the truth and the life' (John 14:5–6, NIV).

Here, again, he is granted one of the most vivid exchanges in the New Testament. It's as if God uses Thomas' plodding, unimaginative nature to reveal the glory. So when he comes eventually to meet Jesus after his resurrection, he no longer needs to put his hands on Jesus' wounds. He has only to encounter him, and he believes.

Knowing this, we can all relate to Thomas' experience. When we meet Jesus—whether it is while reading the Bible, at worship, in prayer, through encounters with inspiring people or whatever—we can join in saying, 'My Lord and my God.'

PRAYER

Father, take my dull, earthbound thoughts and lift them to your glory.

Someone to watch over me

And, behold, two of them went that same day to a village called Emmaus, which was from Jerusalem about threescore furlongs. And they talked together of all these things which had happened. And it came to pass, that, while they communed together and reasoned, Jesus himself drew near, and went with them. But their eyes were holden that they should not know him.

There is a rightly celebrated testimony of how, in his Antarctic expedition of 1914–16, Sir Ernest Shackleton and his team of 28 explorers were stranded in the polar wastes after their ship became trapped in the ice. They faced a risky journey over hundreds of miles to safety.

Remarkably, all survived. More remarkably still, whenever they did a head count, they all had the strong impression that there was an extra man with them. Particularly on the bleakest, most hopeless parts of the journey, when a small group went on ahead, there was an additional, comforting presence. It reassured them that they were not as isolated as they seemed to be.

Many others, too, have experienced the sensation of a supportive figure alongside them in their darkest moments (think of the popularity of the Footprints story, printed on so many prayer cards). Often, we can look back to this passage and see how Jesus came to be with these two disciples.

The two weren't very important characters, not even in the inner circle of apostles, but, in their time of need, Jesus travelled with them.

Just as these disciples didn't recognise Jesus, so we often do not realise that God has been with us all the way. We sometimes look back and wonder, 'How on earth did I get through that?' It is when we reach a later stage of our journey that we can recognise that God was there with us.

This is one of the reasons some people give for the usefulness of keeping a spiritual journal: it can remind them of both good and bad times, in the constant presence of God. The very process of writing things down means that you weigh them up, so that perhaps they don't seem so bleak. Also, if you turn back to old entries later, you might find patterns and signs of hope that you hadn't noticed before.

PRAYER

Lord God, you are with me, now and always, even when it seems hard to sense your presence. Help me to be open to you as I travel along.

Learners on the road

And he said unto them, What manner of communications are these that ye have one to another, as ye walk, and are sad? And the one of them, whose name was Cleopas, answering said unto him, Art thou only a stranger in Jerusalem, and hast not known the things which are come to pass there in these days? And he said unto them, What things? And they said unto him, Concerning Jesus of Nazareth, which was a prophet mighty in deed and word before God and all the people: And how the chief priests and our rulers delivered him to be condemned to death, and have crucified him.

Two disciples are walking together the seven or so miles from Jerusalem to Emmaus, discussing and feeling sad about the events surrounding Jesus' death. They seem to be trying to piece together what has happened, mulling over his life, his trial and crucifixion and, finally, the strange tales of the women and their vision of angels. Confusion reigns. At least they have the comfort of each other: they share the burden, sparking off one another to offer hope, rather than just wallowing in an individual pit of unhappiness and uncertainty.

When they fall into conversation with a stranger, it is revealing to see how they summarise what has happened (vv. 19–24). To them, it was important that Jesus was 'a prophet mighty in deed and word before God and all the people'. Would most people describe him like that now? They might say that he was a fine moral teacher, a good man and a useful, compassionate healer, but they probably wouldn't stress his relationship and status with God quite so prominently.

To the disciples, the fact that God has blessed Jesus is crucial. Even in the midst of their grief and uncertainty (not to mention their uncertainty about scripture, which the stranger has to open up to them), they focus on Jesus' closeness to God. This is, surely, one of the things that makes them ready, so that Jesus can explain the scriptures to them, despite their having been so slow in the past to grasp the message about the Messiah.

They may be 'fools', as Jesus says later on (v. 25), but they are disciples—centred on God in their assessment of Jesus, and wanting to learn. After all, 'disciples' means 'learners'. They have a long way to go but already they are travelling in the right direction.

——— MEDITATION ———

'Commit thy way unto the Lord; trust also in him;
and he shall bring it to pass' (Psalm 37:5).

Sudden moments of illumination

And they drew nigh unto the village, whither they went: and he made as though he would have gone further. But they constrained him, saying, Abide with us: for it is toward evening, and the day is far spent. And he went in to tarry with them. And it came to pass, as he sat at meat with them, he took bread, and blessed it, and brake, and gave to them. And their eyes were opened, and they knew him; and he vanished out of their sight.

We might muddle through life, failing to recognise God with us, both in our times of trouble and in the mundane, boring times when everything drifts by. Suddenly, though, we see him in the breaking of bread. An experience of true worship is sometimes given to us in which we know the Lord is with us. These moments can sustain us through so much. Yet, for most of the time, apart from such special shaft-of-illumination or mountain-top experiences, it can be more a matter of remembering—the type of remembering that was so important to the Israelites as they recalled their deliverance from Egypt. In a similar way, we can recall the facts of what God has already done for us and the amazing grace that he gives us.

In many ways, this is more important than the spiritual highs, for if we rely too much on emotional trips, we are not building on sure foundations. After his resurrection, one of the first things Jesus said was, 'Touch me not' (which is often paraphrased as 'Don't cling to me'), when he met Mary Magdalene in the garden (John 20:17). He seemed to be telling her, among other things, not to keep grasping on to her old view of him, as this might pigeonhole him and belittle his power. We can be guilty of putting other people and situations into little boxes, in an unhelpful way, to make ourselves think we have some sort of control over them.

So often, Jesus slips away just as we recognise him and think we've got him pinned down. Moments of illumination are wonderful gifts but fleeting ones: we shouldn't try to freeze them (as Peter wanted to do by building tabernacles at the transfiguration in Matthew 17:4). Jesus is far greater than our conception of him.

PRAYER

Father, thank you for all the sudden moments of illumination. Strengthen me to keep going whenever I fail to recognise you.

Blessing—a shared experience

And they said one to another, Did not our heart burn within us, while he talked with us by the way, and while he opened to us the scriptures? And they rose up the same hour, and returned to Jerusalem, and found the eleven gathered together, and them that were with them, Saying, The Lord is risen indeed, and hath appeared to Simon. And they told what things were done in the way, and how he was known of them in breaking of bread.

The two disciples are reeling from their astonishing experience. It wasn't just one of them who thought that something very special was going on: they were able to corroborate each other's testimony when they returned to their friends.

This is an unusual experience of blessing in the Bible, as, so often, it is single individuals who are given such illustrations of God's goodness. It can be a lonely road for those who are blessed, as it was for the Old Testament prophets. They have no one who can share their sense of God, and they can feel that they are getting nowhere as they try to communicate their vision to others. However, in this case, the two disciples have each other to turn to. They go back to Jerusalem 'the same hour', eager to tell the others.

What they have been through is like an experience of worship. Their hearts burned as they heard the scriptures opened up to them, and Jesus was made known to them in the breaking of bread.

For many of us, as we meet for worship, the Eucharist balances word and sacrament, so we hear the scriptures and then an explanation of them. Our hearts ought to burn within us as we listen. Then, we have the breaking of the bread—an amazing opportunity to know Jesus and get close to him. Our experience of worship can often fall a long way short of this, but this is what is offered to us every time Holy Communion is celebrated.

--- **REFLECTION** ---

God our Father, you have raised our humanity in Christ, and have fed us with the bread of heaven: mercifully grant that, nourished with such spiritual blessings, we may set our hearts in the heavenly places.
Post-Communion prayer for Ascension Day, *Common Worship*

Clearing away the fear

And as they thus spake, Jesus himself stood in the midst of them, and saith unto them, Peace be unto you. But they were terrified and affrighted, and supposed that they had seen a spirit. And he said unto them, Why are ye troubled? and why do thoughts arise in your hearts? Behold my hands and my feet, that it is I myself: handle me, and see; for a spirit hath not flesh and bones, as ye see me have.

While the disciples struggle to come to terms with the stories of the women at the tomb (Luke 24:9–11) and in Emmaus, suddenly Jesus comes to them. After the puzzling rumours and bizarre tales, his appearance is startling in its directness. He arrives, reassures them and offers convincing proof of his solid flesh. He meets their fears head on: 'Handle me, and see' (v. 39). As so often, the KJV word 'handle' suggests a raw physicality that other translations, which use words such as 'touch', don't quite reach.

It is interesting that he tackles their anxiety and disbelief first, before explaining his mission in more detail. He doesn't buffet them with scripture before he has met and then transformed their fears. As a model for evangelism, this approach appeals to many of us. You have to face people honestly first, with all their worries and misconceptions. Even then, you have to acknowledge that they still might not believe in the truth of what you are saying. As we shall see in the next reading, Jesus showed them he was alive by eating fish 'while they yet believed not' (v. 41).

So Jesus acts first to reassure the disciples. With the Holy Spirit, he is able to transform them from an anxious little group, huddled together in fear, to a confident team with the conviction to go out and pass on his message throughout the world. He can equip us like this, too, if we are open to him. We don't have to remain in our fears or leave others in theirs, either. We can all approach the risen Christ.

MEDITATION

Jesus the Son of God is a high priest 'in all points tempted like as we are, yet without sin. Let us therefore come boldly unto the throne of grace, that we may obtain mercy, and find grace to help in time of need' (Hebrews 4:15–16).

Too solid flesh

And when he had thus spoken, he shewed them his hands and his feet. And while they yet believed not for joy, and wondered, he said unto them, Have ye here any meat? And they gave him a piece of a broiled fish, and of an honeycomb. And he took it, and did eat before them.

To prove that he is no ghost or spirit, Jesus does something amazing: he eats a piece of fish. Such an everyday thing—the natural satisfying of appetite—is invested with enormous significance because of who he is. I remember seeing this event dramatised as part of the National Theatre's production of *The Mysteries*, a version of the medieval mystery plays. From the great mass of material available, the dramatist and poet Tony Harrison chose to highlight this episode.

The sheer wonder of it was dwelt on at some length in the production, even to the point of appearing slightly awkward: the disciples gasped in amazement as Jesus chewed. Why was his eating so important? It proved that he had a physical body and wasn't just an apparition. Some people might have thought he was a spirit, without substance, especially given his ability to turn up behind locked doors (John 20:19) and vanish suddenly (Luke 24:31), but this shows that Jesus' resurrection body—wounds and all—was solid stuff.

He wasn't just a projection in the minds of the frightened disciples, in the way that many bereaved people imagine they see again someone who has just died. That is a natural enough reaction to loss and the intense focus of grief. Jesus' resurrection, on the other hand, was a once-for-all physical happening—proof of the triumph over death in which we can all share.

Yet this solid resurrection was more than a one-off event, for its implications are still with us. However much we may think that things are dead and buried, God can still raise them to new life. There may be relationships, plans and hopes that seem to have come to the end of their life, but God can still raise them up and make them new.

MEDITATION

Who would have thought my shrivelled heart
Could have recovered greenness? It was gone
Quite underground...
These are thy wonders, Lord of love,
To make us see we are but flowers that glide;
Which when we once can find and prove,
Thou hast a garden for us, where to bide.

George Herbert, 'The Flower'

Repentance and forgiveness together

Then opened he their understanding, that they might understand
the scriptures, And said unto them, Thus it is written, and thus it
behoved Christ to suffer, and to rise from the dead the third day:
And that repentance and remission of sins should be preached in
his name among all nations, beginning at Jerusalem. And ye are witnesses of these things. And, behold, I send the promise of my Father
upon you: but tarry ye in the city of Jerusalem, until ye be endued
with power from on high.

At last, the disciples are starting to realise that Jesus really is alive, so he
can begin to tell them more and give them some solid nourishment. He
opens their minds to understand the scriptures. It leads up to the goal 'that
repentance and remission of sins should be preached in his name' (v. 47).

This is our work, the upshot of Jesus' mission. We have to offer to the
world the chance to clear away its sins and be forgiven. The two ideas,
repentance and remission (or, as we would say now, forgiveness), are
inseparable, but it's easy to focus on one at the expense of the other. Many
misconceptions about Christianity seem to stem from either an undue
focus on aspects of repentance—all sin and wickedness, wallowing in guilt
and picking over past wrongs—or forgiveness—all easy, feel-good uplift,
without any sense of personal responsibility.

Although we might tire of Christians' media image as, on the one hand,
gloom and judgment merchants and, on the other, superficial happy-clap-
pies, Jesus calls us to proclaim repentance and forgiveness at the same time.
We need to find fresh ways of doing this that reach people now, appealing
to them as they are but also drawing them on further, towards God. We
need to include both repentance—turning away from what we know in our
hearts is wrong and selfish—and forgiveness, turning towards God in the
assurance of his love for each of us.

Of course, we are not left to do this by our own efforts, however determined they are. Jesus promises that we will be 'endued with power from
on high'. We wait for the coming of the Spirit.

--- REFLECTION ---

'I will not leave you comfortless: I will come to you' (John 14:18).

The cloud of unknowing

And when he had spoken these things, while they beheld, he was taken up; and a cloud received him out of their sight. And while they looked stedfastly toward heaven as he went up, behold, two men stood by them in white apparel; Which also said, Ye men of Galilee, why stand ye gazing up into heaven? this same Jesus, which is taken up from you into heaven, shall so come in like manner as ye have seen him go into heaven.

On Ascension Day, we celebrate Jesus' leaving the earth and returning to the Father in heaven. He had to move on from being with his disciples on earth, after he had risen from the dead, so that the Holy Spirit could come. Naturally, it was hard on the disciples at the time. The two men in white ask them, 'Why stand ye gazing up into heaven?'

As so often during Jesus' earthly ministry, the disciples seem a bit slow on the uptake. They often used to misunderstand what he had come for, wondering whether his kingdom was of this world. Here, they gaze up into the sky. I imagine them gawping, open-mouthed, probably looking a bit silly.

Reading it now, of course, we are in a much better position than they were to understand what is going on. We know that the next episode in the story is the triumphant experience of Pentecost. Perhaps we shouldn't let that make us feel too smug, however. It could remind us of those times when we had little or no clue about what might be going on in our Christian life, when we wondered why God seemed to have been taken from us.

The disciples had to go through this experience in order that they might know God in a fuller, more powerful way. Such times, when God seems to be hidden by clouds of unknowing, are a step in our progress towards a deeper relationship with the Father. Some give up at this stage, disheartened by their lack of warm, spiritual feelings. But this is a recognised part of the spiritual journey, attested by many Christians over the centuries. In its extreme form, it is the 'dark night of the soul' and can continue for agonising years. If we persevere, though, secure in the knowledge that God is with us, we shall enter, eventually, into a new dimension of knowing and loving him.

--- PRAYER ---

Father, help me to overcome my fears about your absence. Grant that I may know that you are with me always, no matter now I feel.

Constant prayer and housekeeping

Then returned they unto Jerusalem from the mount called Olivet, which is from Jerusalem a sabbath day's journey. And when they were come in, they went up into an upper room, where abode both Peter, and James, and John, and Andrew, Philip, and Thomas, Bartholomew, and Matthew, James the son of Alphaeus, and Simon Zelotes, and Judas the brother of James. These all continued with one accord in prayer and supplication, with the women, and Mary the mother of Jesus, and with his brethren.

This passage refers to what has become a strange and special time in the Christian year, the nine days between Ascension and Pentecost. They are odd, in-between days, coming after one triumphant departure and before another spectacular demonstration of God's power. So what do the disciples do? They 'all continued with one accord in prayer and supplication'. There is a tremendous sense of expectation, and not just because we, reading this so much later, know what happens next. The next few verses (vv. 15–26) also tell us that they used the time profitably in choosing a successor to Judas Iscariot, to take the number of the apostles back up to twelve.

For us, these nine days can become a tremendous opportunity, if we can make the time somehow to spend more time in prayer, in expectation of the Holy Spirit. Equally, they can become a fruitless period of waiting, hanging around for the next big event to happen. The choice is ours.

These days can be seen as a parable of the whole of our Christian life. Like the disciples at the time of the ascension, we have been assured of God's presence ('I am with you alway', Matthew 28:20), but there is a time lag before we are given the full experience of God.

There are those of us who don't find prayer easy, for whom the idea of constant devotion to prayer perhaps makes us think that it might have been all very well for the disciples, but not for us. Maybe this is where the choosing of a replacement apostle comes in. As we know, the Christian life isn't only one of unceasing prayer, even for those in monasteries. There is also the 'housekeeping'—a whole range of tasks that are needed to keep the show on the road. They may be a trivial round of administration and sheer drudgery, especially in churches and Christian organisations, but there are some jobs that have to be done. They, too, have their place in the life of Christians waiting on the Lord.

--- **PRAYER** ---

Lord, help me to balance prayer and daily work as I wait expectantly on you.

Above us and alongside us

Then the eleven disciples went away into Galilee, into a mountain where Jesus had appointed them. And when they saw him, they worshipped him: but some doubted. And Jesus came and spake unto them, saying, All power is given unto me in heaven and in earth. Go ye therefore, and teach all nations, baptising them in the name of the Father, and of the Son, and of the Holy Ghost: Teaching them to observe all things whatsoever I have commanded you: and, lo, I am with you alway, even unto the end of the world. Amen.

When the disciples saw Jesus, there on the mountain where he had told them to meet him, they worshipped him. The verse seems to imply that they all worshipped, even those who were doubtful about the whole business. Presumably the experience, the sight of Jesus back from the dead, was so overwhelming that they could barely believe their eyes. They were awestruck and could hardly help themselves from paying homage.

This sense of awe can be hard for us to recover today. It can be difficult to catch it in worship (especially in some churches) and we might also share some of the disciples' doubts. On those seemingly all-too-rare occasions when we are given a glimpse of the overwhelming majesty of God, it can be hard to square the mountain-top experience with our sense of Jesus as a human, like us, suffering alongside us. Here, though, in the same passage, is an assurance of that fact: 'I am with you alway' (v. 20). Here are both the awe-inspiring glory of God and the comforting closeness of the man who has tasted pain like ours. Jesus is fully God and fully human. The two senses of God's presence cannot be separated.

It is the assurance of the Lord, both above us and alongside us, transcendent and immanent, that gives us what we need to go out and make disciples. We are sent out with the authority of God, who is with us to the end of time. Having this strength and inner confidence on our side, we can pass the message on.

PRAYER

Lord of the heights and depths, grant me a sense of your presence with me in all that I do today.

Richard of Chichester

These readings are written as an introduction to Richard of Chichester, the laughing but hair-shirted bishop who, appropriately, is best known now for one of his prayers. Richard (c. 1197–1253) was famous for being happy. He sounds like a Friar Tuck type—full of laughter and very hospitable. Many of the stories we have about him come from his friend and confessor, Friar Ralph Bocking. Friar Ralph describes how the people of Sussex, to whom Richard ministered, made a joke of his name, Ricardus—standing for 'RIdens, CARus, DUlcis', meaning 'laughing, beloved, sweet'.

This didn't mean that he was superficial. His good humour was bound up with his love of Jesus and his overwhelming sense of gratitude for what his redeemer and friend had done. This is reflected in his celebrated prayer:

Thanks be to thee, our Lord Jesus Christ, for all the benefits which thou hast given me, for all the pains and insults which thou hast borne for me. O most merciful Redeemer, Friend, and Brother, may I know thee more clearly, love thee more dearly, and follow thee more nearly. Amen

The first sentence of the prayer comes from Richard himself: they are words that he spoke on his deathbed. The rest was added later (probably in the early 20th century), inspired by his outlook and influence. The phrase 'day by day' seems to have been attached to the end even later. It is, of course, famous from the musical *Godspell*, where it was turned into a song.

It can seem disappointing that the entire prayer isn't by the man himself, but I think it's important to be realistic about what has survived over so many centuries and grateful for one individual's continuing legacy.

Richard was born into a prosperous farming family in Droitwich, Worcestershire. He turned away from the family business to study at Oxford and later at Paris and Bologna. He became Chancellor of Oxford University—its head—and it wasn't until later that he became a priest. There was a dispute when he was made a bishop, as King Henry III preferred another candidate and refused to give him his lands or home for two years (the Crown held the property when there was a vacancy). He was bishop for only eight years but he made a huge impact. He was strict with his clergy but also with himself, and cared greatly for the poor and sick.

God's guiding hand in the wilderness

Behold, I go forward, but he is not there; and backward, but I cannot perceive him: On the left hand, where he doth work, but I cannot behold him: he hideth himself on the right hand, that I cannot see him: But he knoweth the way that I take: when he hath tried me, I shall come forth as gold. My foot hath held his steps, his way have I kept, and not declined... For he performeth the thing that is appointed for me.

It's far too easy with hindsight to see Richard's life as one of triumph, as he was a firm but fair man, ministering to his flock, who loved him dearly. However, there were many times—including periods of whole years—when it wasn't like that at all for him. It must have seemed as if he would never get the chance even to begin his work properly when he spent two years at the beginning of his time as a bishop relying on handouts and hospitality, as the king refused to give him the home that went with his post.

Richard might well have felt as if God was hiding himself, as Job felt in this passage. We could understand it if Richard felt lonely, isolated, even abandoned by God, but perhaps he was able to look back to an even bleaker experience in his life and see that God had not vanished, even if he couldn't feel the warm glow of his presence at that point. I'm thinking of the time in Richard's early life when he had to leave his studies at Oxford and return to help with the family farm after his father's death. This sometimes happens in families. It often seems to be women who end up leaving their study or paid work in order to keep the home going. Some have to cope with this disappointment for the whole of their lives. It might well have seemed as if he would never get the chance to have his own life, but Richard managed to return to university and, eventually, to become a priest. He trusted that God would complete what he had appointed for him, somehow (v. 14).

--- REFLECTION ---

We do not need to be very old to look back on life and see that things that we thought were disasters worked out to our good... we can see a guiding and a directing hand in it.

William Barclay

God's love reaches beyond death

God standeth in the congregation of the mighty; he judgeth among the gods. How long will ye judge unjustly, and accept the persons of the wicked? ... Deliver the poor and needy: rid them out of the hand of the wicked... Arise, O God, judge the earth: for thou shalt inherit all nations.

———————————

It was on 16 June 1276 that St Richard's body was moved a few yards from a chapel at Chichester Cathedral to a shrine behind the high altar. He had been dead for 23 years at that point and was already recognised as a saint, so the new site became a place of pilgrimage, and the date became St Richard's Day. The fact that we celebrate Richard on this day rather than on the day of his birth, death or other significant event in his life reflects why he is important. He has had a life since his death that has mattered as much, if not more, than anything he might have achieved in this world— both in the way he affected others' lives as an inspiration to them and in his eternal life in God's presence. He has a relationship with God that never ends. Such relationships in God's love, in this world and the next, are the building blocks of the world.

This psalm above sets up a contrast between God's values and those of the world. It imagines God in a sort of heavenly council, giving judgment among other gods. God accuses the worldly gods of being unjust and favouring the wicked (v. 2), but he, the one true God, is different: he wants to 'deliver the poor and needy' (v. 4). Richard was famed for his generosity to poor people—so much so that his financial advisers begged him to stop giving so much away as he was leaving nothing in the church's resources. When he visited his flock, he would seek out the poor and sick, seeing them personally and giving them food.

The Old Testament constantly reminds us that God favours the poor and weak, yet we still struggle to recall this every day. We need to be told how the universe really functions—how it is undergirded by God—as, otherwise, the worldly notions of 'every man for himself' can easily and insidiously creep in. That is why the habits of regular prayer, reading, reflection and worship are so important. They return us to the reality of God's rule.

——————— **PRAYER** ———————

Father, help me to realise today that you judge the earth (Psalm 82:8).

Being content in plenty and in need

Not that I speak in respect of want: for I have learned, in whatsoever state I am, therewith to be content. I know both how to be abased, and I know how to abound: every where and in all things I am instructed both to be full and to be hungry, both to abound and to suffer need. I can do all things through Christ which strengtheneth me.

Developing the theme in the previous reading of God's values overturning those of the world, here is Paul thanking the Philippians for their support of his ministry. He is looking beyond the basic needs of survival and the desire to have more than enough, in the search for God's ideas of plenty. The KJV's 'to be abased' and 'to abound' can also be translated 'to have little' and 'to have plenty'.

Jesus never promises that his followers will be rich, but he does promise that they might have life 'more abundantly' (John 10:10). It reminds me of my favourite film, *I Know Where I'm Going*, released in 1945. In the Western Isles of Scotland, Joan (a stranger) observes to the local laird, 'People around here are very poor, I suppose.' He replies, 'Not poor; they just haven't got money.' 'It's the same thing,' she argues. 'Oh, no, it's something quite different.' Among the many things that happen in the film, Joan comes to realise that cash isn't the answer to everything.

In a similar way, after he spent his first years as a bishop homeless and without money, Richard had to go from having absolutely nothing, relying on others to feed and house him, to living in a bishop's palace and having enough to give away—even if his staff disapproved. Like Paul, he must have been instructed by these things 'both to be full and to be hungry' (v. 12). The lesson he learnt was to rely on God.

Such reliance isn't the idle irresponsibility of not working for your living and expecting that you and your family can survive on air, but the realisation that feast or famine don't matter in themselves. If you are alive with just about enough to eat and a roof over your head, the important thing is that the whole of life is a wonderful gift from God, for which we should be grateful.

--- **REFLECTION** ---

Thank God, carefully and wonderingly, for your continuing privileges, and for every experience of his goodness. Thankfulness is a soil in which pride does not easily grow.

Archbishop Michael Ramsey (1904–88)

Find rest unto your souls

At that time Jesus answered and said, I thank thee, O Father, Lord
of heaven and earth, because thou hast hid these things from the
wise and prudent, and hast revealed them unto babes... Come unto
me, all ye that labour and are heavy laden, and I will give you rest.
Take my yoke upon you, and learn of me; for I am meek and lowly
in heart: and ye shall find rest unto your souls. For my yoke is easy,
and my burden is light.

This is the type of passage that is crystal clear in the KJV, which might
have given Richard the assurance he needed to defy the king. He realised that the king could, and did, deprive him of his home and possessions
and could have done even worse than that. He wasn't anxious, though,
because he knew that God was ultimately the one in control.

Richard saw the necessity of keeping to God's ways, not giving up
in despair, even if others might have felt that God had abandoned him.
Richard was known for spending hours in private prayer, opening himself
up to God's will every day. Those who knew him reported that he would
often get up very early, while the rest of the household (including his chap-
lains) was still asleep, and tiptoe to the chapel to pray before the business
of the day began. He would tell himself off if the birds were already singing
before he was up and praising God.

Such a quiet, regular habit, going on in an unshowy way, requires tremendous self-discipline to sustain, even though, to someone looking in
from outside, nothing much seems to be happening. It's this kind of steady,
regular prayer, this daily offering to God, that provides the spiritual food
needed to sustain us throughout the day. Without it, we are blown by every
wind of circumstance and others' demands, and have no sense of our own
centre with God. It's when we know that we're loved and have taken the
time to feel God's hand on our day that we can behave and respond in an
honest way that reflects the truth of God in our lives.

--- REFLECTION ---

If we are to follow Christ, it must be in our common way of spending every day.
William Law, *A Serious Call to a Devout and Holy Life* (1728)

Jesus our loving friend and brother

This is my commandment, That ye love one another, as I have loved
you. Greater love hath no man than this, that a man lay down his
life for his friends. Ye are my friends, if ye do whatsoever I command
you. Henceforth I call you not servants; for the servant knoweth not
what his lord doeth: but I have called you friends; for all things that I
have heard of my Father I have made known unto you... These things
I command you, that ye love one another.

This passage is about a Lord who takes us into his confidence, who
believes in us so much that he shares his insights and hopes with us.
He makes us his friends.

It is appropriate for our reflections on Richard because of the following words from his famous prayer: 'O most merciful redeemer, friend and
brother'. As we saw in the Introduction, these words were added after he
died, but were written in the spirit of his devotion to reflect his particular
approach. They seem to refer to the above Gospel passage, not just because
they include the word 'friend' but also because of the ending of the prayer
about loving God more clearly, dearly and nearly. Knowing Jesus more
clearly relates to the contrast Jesus himself makes between a friend and a
servant, who does not know what his Lord does. Loving him more dearly
picks up on the main point of the passage (vv. 12, 17), that we love one
another; while following more nearly corresponds to the whole idea of the
intimacy of our relationships with friends and therefore our closeness to
God.

One of the reasons for the special power St Richard's prayer has to
move people is the way it places side by side our gratefulness to Jesus for
the heart-stopping love he has shown us in bearing so much pain, with the
hope that this might spur us on in three specific areas, to which we can
easily relate. We move from our gratitude to our wish to know him more,
which will lead inevitably to our loving him more. This, in turn, will enable
us to follow him more closely. It's a simple progression that forms a journey
of the heart: thankfulness to knowledge to love to follow-up in action. Jesus
draws us into this, gently and lovingly, by inviting us to be his friends.

--- **REFLECTION** ---

*The love and the thankfulness seem straightforward and easy enough, but what
are you doing today to follow your friend Jesus more nearly?*

Lovest thou me?

So when they had dined, Jesus saith to Simon Peter, Simon, son of Jonas, lovest thou me more than these? He saith unto him, Yea, Lord; thou knowest that I love thee. He saith unto him, Feed my lambs. He saith to him again the second time, Simon, son of Jonas, lovest thou me? He saith unto him, Yea, Lord; thou knowest that I love thee. He saith unto him, Feed my sheep. He saith unto him the third time, Simon, son of Jonas, lovest thou me? Peter was grieved because he said unto him the third time, Lovest thou me?

Our final passage, divided between this and the next reading, shows Jesus after his resurrection, grilling Peter about what is going to happen next. Jesus isn't just asking whether Peter really loves him, but what that love means—how much it will enable him to endure. Among other things, Jesus is saying that this love can't be merely a warm, cosy feeling or a sentimental gesture. This is a gift, but one that involves a difficult, grown-up response and a task—feeding the flock.

It is a fitting message in relation to Richard because of the way he combined the personal warmth and joy of love with a tough discipline. He was strict—most of all with himself, in that he dressed plainly, ate simply and didn't indulge in politics, gossip and ego trips (unlike many of his fellow bishops and, perhaps, even some bishops today). However, he could also demand nearly as much from others. He set high standards and sacked those who flouted them by acting immorally and dishonestly. He dismissed one guilty priest, despite appeals from powerful people, including the king and queen, who could have made life difficult for him (as we have seen).

It can seem hard (as it was for Peter here, when he felt aggrieved that Jesus asked the same question three times) to connect the two faces of love that we see in those who cherish us—the affectionate generosity and the mature response to the imperfections of the beloved. However, they do belong together and each will gain from being part of the larger whole.

--- **REFLECTION** ---

Love is eager, sincere and kind; it is glad and lovely; it is strong, patient and faithful; wise, long-suffering and resolute; and it never seeks its own ends, for where a man seeks his own ends, he at once falls out of love.
Thomas à Kempis, *The Imitation of Christ* (c. 1418)

What are you doing about this love?

And [Peter] said unto him, Lord, thou knowest all things; thou knowest that I love thee. Jesus saith unto him, Feed my sheep. Verily, verily, I say unto thee, When thou wast young, thou girdedst thyself, and walkedst whither thou wouldest: but when thou shalt be old, thou shalt stretch forth thy hands, and another shall gird thee, and carry thee whither thou wouldest not. This spake he, signifying by what death he should glorify God. And when he had spoken this, he saith unto him, Follow me.

This second half of the passage we started to look at in the previous reading elaborates on the mature response to God's amazing love and tremendous gifts. Jesus describes how hard it will be to feed the flock. Also, his final words, 'Follow me', will take Peter to his own cross.

As we saw earlier, Jesus' words reflect the pattern of Richard's most famous prayer (see the Introduction to this section of readings to remind yourself of the full prayer). It starts with thankfulness to God for what he has done and leads, inevitably, through knowledge and love to our response of following Jesus. Yes, Jesus knows that we love him, but it's as if he looks us steadily in the eye and asks what we are going to do about it.

We have to keep asking ourselves this question, just as Jesus kept on asking Peter. Like Richard, we need to keep the laughter and the hard graft of discipline bound together, day by day. We can do this by means of regular prayer and active, generous concern for the needy, as Richard did. We know that God will sustain us when we do this consistently, even if it doesn't seem convenient or we don't feel like doing it.

We needn't feel disheartened that Richard was holier than us: the people who knew him didn't worry about that. Instead, we should recall and appreciate those qualities of warmth and closeness to God that made him both a saint and a greatly loved man who showed his friends the way to the Lord.

REFLECTION

A saint is a human creature devoured and transformed by love: a love that has dissolved and burnt out those instinctive passions—acquisitive and combative, proud and greedy—which commonly rule the lives of men.

Evelyn Underhill (1875–1941)

Julian of Norwich

When I think of Julian of Norwich, three passages from her *Revelations of Divine Love* immediately spring to mind. First, her most celebrated words, 'all shall be well and all manner of thing shall be well'; second, her neat, telling image of a nut: 'a little thing, the size of a hazelnut... It is all that is made... it will last for ever because God loves it'; and, third, more difficult to summarise, her wisdom about suffering.

We don't know the real name of the writer who called herself Julian of Norwich, or much about her, for certain. She was born in about 1342, within a couple of years of the poet Geoffrey Chaucer. Some think she was a Benedictine nun, but it is known that, when she was quite a mature woman, she went to live in a room attached to the church of St Julian in Norwich and took her name from it.

In May 1373, when she was about 30 and thought to be dying, she experienced 16 visions, which revealed to her aspects of God's love. She spent the next 20 years trying to work out what they meant. She wrote down what she had seen and thought, and her book is the earliest to survive by a woman in English. This set her apart as not just a visionary with great spiritual insight but also a serious theologian. She devoted her life to prayer and giving spiritual guidance to her many visitors.

Her work was rediscovered during the 20th century, and T.S. Eliot quoted her in his long poem 'Little Gidding', at the culmination of his great *Four Quartets*. Now, she has become genuinely popular. People who don't know anything about medieval literature and theology have sensed that her words address their innermost needs. She speaks directly to the concerns of the heart and the worries we all have about big questions such as suffering.

I have chosen seven Bible passages, spread over twelve readings. The first four are the ones set out to commemorate her in *Exciting Holiness*, a book of readings for the Church's lesser festivals compiled by Brother Tristam SSF (Canterbury Press, 2003).

Julian's writing is available in many different types of books: there are pocket-sized short extracts in *Enfolded in Love* and *In Love Enclosed*, both by Robert Llewellyn (DLT, 2004), full translations of her work in *The Revelations of Divine Love* by A.C. Spearing and Elizabeth Spearing (Penguin, 1998) and *Showing of Love*, translated by Julia Bolton Holloway (DLT, 2003), as well as books about her, such as *In Search of Julian of Norwich* by Sheila Upjohn (DLT, 1989).

God is there at your lowest point

And he came thither unto a cave, and lodged there; and, behold, the word of the Lord came to him, and he said unto him, What doest thou here, Elijah? And he said, I have been very jealous for the Lord God of hosts: for the children of Israel have forsaken thy covenant, thrown down thine altars, and slain thy prophets with the sword; and I, even I only, am left; and they seek my life, to take it away.

In this and the next passage, we're looking at the Old Testament lesson chosen to commemorate Julian of Norwich. I imagine this famous passage, which builds to its climax in the next reading with the 'still small voice', was seen as appropriate for someone who experienced a vision of God while alone. Julian writes that her 'showings of God' came to her between four and nine in the morning. This wasn't a social experience, but something given to her alone and individually.

The contrast with Elijah is telling. At this point in the first book of Kings, he is running away from King Ahab and Queen Jezebel (19:2–3)—which is understandable, as they are trying to kill him. He is lonely and (not surprisingly) feeling sorry for himself. He sees himself as having been faithful to the Lord, but where has it got him? Now he's the only one left. Who could be more isolated? God, however, has other ideas, as we shall see in the next reading.

Julian of Norwich, on the other hand, was actively seeking God. When she believed that she was on her deathbed, she prayed to see Jesus' passion (his suffering). Unlike Elijah, she wasn't running away and she didn't resort to desperate self-justification, saying how good she had been. Both Julian and Elijah thought that they were in danger of dying, but Julian embraced the idea. She was concentrating on the essentials as her time came near. In times of crisis like this, our true colours are revealed. I fear that I'd be more like Elijah and run away.

What Julian and Elijah have in common, though, is that this lowest ebb, when they thought life couldn't get any worse, was a turning point. Both were rewarded by God with a vision.

--- **PRAYER** ---

Father, give me the strength to face the things that terrify me, including death, and to remember that I am enfolded in your love.

Searching for God

And, behold, the Lord passed by, and a great and strong wind rent the mountains, and brake in pieces the rocks before the Lord; but the Lord was not in the wind: and after the wind an earthquake; but the Lord was not in the earthquake: And after the earthquake a fire; but the Lord was not in the fire: and after the fire a still small voice.

God granted Elijah a physical sense of his presence—'a still small voice', so much more vivid than other translations' 'a sound of sheer silence' and 'the sound of a gentle whisper'. Julian, on the other hand, was given a vision of Jesus, Mary and various other things, such as her famous image of the hazelnut, and assurances of God's love0. Some people will instinctively doubt these experiences and put them down to hallucinations or illness. Whatever our view, the point of these gifts is that God is doing something way out of the ordinary: he is speaking to his followers in a very unusual way.

Neither Elijah nor Julian took their experience for granted. People who draw close to God are not looking for such miracles: if they were thrill-seekers, they would have fallen away long before. So here are special gifts of vision, freely offered and undeserved, like grace. Julian received hers in a spirit of steady thankfulness, knowing that it was not a reward for any special goodness.

This might seem a long way from our own lives. Elijah and Julian are hardly everyday role models for 21st-century people, and the whole idea of visions is an aspect of the religious life that we might be almost embarrassed about. God, though, gives us all insights into his love. He might not have granted us an extraordinary experience, but each day he gives us some sense of his presence, if we can find him. Every time you're struck afresh by God's goodness, love or sheer wonder, isn't that the Holy Spirit giving you a tiny reflection of the type of experience Elijah and Julian had? Perhaps you've found this in the beauty of God's creation or the love of your family or friends, or as some truth from the Bible leaps out at you. You don't have to be clever or even particularly holy: God still gives a sense of himself. Every one of us has our own little visions, however fleeting.

--- **PRAYER** ---

Father, thank you for showing yourself to us in so many ways.

You shall not be overcome

The Lord is my light and my salvation; whom shall I fear? the Lord is the strength of my life; of whom shall I be afraid? When the wicked, even mine enemies and my foes, came upon me to eat up my flesh, they stumbled and fell. Though an host should encamp against me, my heart shall not fear: though war should rise against me, in this will I be confident.

If, in the previous reading, we heard about the vision, here is the effect of the vision. The gift has been given for several purposes. Julian is a good example of the type of person the psalmist is writing about. After her visions, she was confident in her faith. She had lost any timorous hesitancy—as you can tell by looking at the first, shorter version of her book and the second, much longer one. The later version is more assured, in a healthy way. She puts forward her wisdom without arrogance, but also without the fluttery 'little me' defensiveness that can afflict Christians when they think they ought to demonstrate humility. I imagine her being down-to-earth in her spiritual advice to her visitors, not wasting time with false modesty.

Despite being a lone woman in the male-dominated society of her time, Julian shows a fearlessness that reflects her trust in God. She was not frightened of other people, nor of the things that scare so many, such as death and judgment, as we saw in the reading about Elijah running away (1 Kings 19:9–10). Hers is a message of trust, as when she says, '[God] did not say, "You shall not be tormented, you shall not be troubled, you shall not be grieved," but he said, "You shall not be overcome."'

These words have reassured thousands of people—and not in a cheap, comfort-blanket way that pretends everything is OK really, when it might not be. No, Julian's is a way that acknowledges the pain we all face. Surely this is a message that we can share in a sensitive way, without being intrusive, with our friends who are troubled, perhaps particularly those in the later stages of mourning. Julian describes how God says these words 'very loudly and clearly, for security and comfort against all the tribulations that may come'. The torment is still there, but so is God to help us.

REFLECTION

When you have been grieving for a loss, have you ever felt that God was bearing you up?

God wraps us in love

One thing have I desired of the Lord, that will I seek after; that I may dwell in the house of the Lord all the days of my life, to behold the beauty of the Lord, and to inquire in his temple. For in the time of trouble he shall hide me in his pavilion: in the secret of his tabernacle shall he hide me; he shall set me up upon a rock. And now shall mine head be lifted up above mine enemies round about me: therefore will I offer in his tabernacle sacrifices of joy; I will sing, yea, I will sing praises unto the Lord.

These verses reflect Julian's longing for God—one of the most striking aspects of her writing. Of course, it is appropriate that we show our love for our heavenly Father, but the amazing warmth of Julian's devotion bursts through her writing, like sunshine through clouds. It's like seeing two people in love. I remember meeting a glamorous couple who were like this, both successful in their respective professions. Despite their high-profile jobs, which brought public scrutiny and pressure, they were obviously besotted with one another, holding hands as we ate dinner, yet not so absorbed as to exclude everyone else.

In a similar way, Julian delights in the presence of the Lord. She describes his 'familiar love' ('homely loveing' in medieval English): 'He is our clothing, wrapping us for love, embracing and enclosing us ['all beclosyth us'] for tender love, so that he can never leave us, being himself everything that is good for us.' This is the absolute security of our home with God—his temple, shelter and dwelling, as the psalm says—from which we can look out and face the world.

Scientific studies suggest that young children who have had plenty of affection and cuddles aren't fearful to venture out. They're keen to explore the world and not anxious, having experienced the security of home. This isn't about being smug; rather, it's about having firm foundations of love. From this base, we can face almost anything. Our relationship with God can be like this.

Julian writes of how we can find this home by turning to God in prayer. She reports God saying to her, 'I am glad you have come to rest, for I have always loved you, and love you now, and you love me.'

--- PRAYER ---

Father, thank you, thank you for your tender love,
wrapping me in warm affection.

Love was his meaning

Though I speak with the tongues of men and of angels, and have not charity, I am become as sounding brass, or a tinkling cymbal... Charity never faileth: but whether there be prophecies, they shall fail; whether there be tongues, they shall cease; whether there be knowledge, it shall vanish away. For we know in part, and we prophesy in part. But when that which is perfect is come, then that which is in part shall be done away.

It's easy to see why those who compiled readings to commemorate Julian came up with Paul's great tribute to love—this passage, which is one of the most celebrated in the KJV. One of Julian's best-known sentences, even making it to the largely secular *Concise Oxford Dictionary of Quotations*, is, 'Love is our Lord's meaning.'

Julian's writing is like one long commentary on 'Charity never faileth' ('Love never ends' in modern translations). She writes of God being like a loving father or mother who never gives up on his or her child. Julian takes it beyond the sense of the way children always test the strength of parents' love, though. 'You'll still love me, even if I'm really, really naughty?' asked our son when he was six. He knows that we will.

Julian takes the idea further, and looks specifically at the question of our having faith, hope and love, while God remains mysterious. Hence she describes having faith, hope and love 'in reality, but I could not feel them in my heart', after contrasting experiences of joy and sadness—both sent by God. She believed that God's purpose is 'to teach me that it is necessary for everybody to have such experiences, sometimes to be strengthened, sometimes to falter and be left by himself. God... loves us as much in sorrow as in joy... both come from love.' She concludes that 'bliss lasts eternally, and pain passes and shall vanish completely'.

Here and elsewhere, she refers to suffering as being transient, though she doesn't minimise its horror. For her, it is insignificant compared to the far greater joy that we shall have in heaven with God. His love is his ultimate purpose—his meaning all the time, even when we are weighed down by pain, and don't understand why. Even when we don't feel it, we can know—and remember from previous experiences—that God really is with us.

REFLECTION

What will your love mean today?

Being completely known by God

When I was a child, I spake as a child, I understood as a child, I thought as a child: but when I became a man, I put away childish things. For now we see through a glass, darkly; but then face to face: now I know in part; but then shall I know even as also I am known.

As we saw in the previous reading, Julian conveys a strong sense of heaven as being the place where we are united with God in joy. All our questions will be answered and all our anxieties resolved, she assures us. That idea is also reflected in this celebrated Bible passage. Both Paul and Julian had a sense of deep-reaching trust in our heavenly Father. They knew him and were keen to explore further. Neither was cowed into a submissiveness that denied their intelligence and integrity. Both realised, however, that, despite their questioning and use of God-given cleverness, there were things that they would never know in this world. This can sound too close to blind obedience for modern tastes, but going this far was radical in its time.

Hence Julian says, 'And thus our good Lord answered all the questions and doubts I could put forward, saying most comfortingly as follows: "I will make all things well" … It is God's wish that we should know in general terms that all shall be well; but it is not God's wish that we should understand it now, except as much as is suitable for us at the present time.'

Like Paul, she links this idea specifically with God's love, when she says elsewhere, 'This is [Christ's] thirst: a love-longing to have us all together, wholly in himself for his delight; for we are not now as wholly in him as we shall be then.' This is like Paul's 'being known'. Julian declares that 'there neither can nor shall be anything at all between God and man's soul'; we are 'united in this union and made holy in this holiness'.

Julian shared something like St Augustine's sense that God has made us for himself and our souls are restless until they rest in him. So it is that she writes, 'Before he made us, he loved us, and when we were made, we loved him.'

--- PRAYER ---

Father, you know me fully: grant me a greater sense of my dwelling in you.

All shall be well

But Mary stood without at the sepulchre weeping: and as she wept, she stooped down, and looked into the sepulchre, And seeth two angels in white sitting, the one at the head, and the other at the feet, where the body of Jesus had lain. And they say unto her, Woman, why weepest thou? She saith unto them, Because they have taken away my Lord, and I know not where they have laid him. And when she had thus said, she turned herself back, and saw Jesus standing, and knew not that it was Jesus. Jesus saith unto her, Woman, why weepest thou? whom seekest thou?

Like Mary Magdalene here, Julian was familiar with grief. Her visions came to her when she was so ill that she and everyone else assumed she would die. As we saw in the reading from 1 Corinthians 13, she had a strong sense that pain is short-lived compared to the endless bliss of heaven, but she still knew that pain is real: 'All this life and this distress which we have here is only a moment, and when we are suddenly taken from suffering into bliss, then the suffering will be nothing.'

God reassures her with the words, '"All manner of things shall be well"; for he wants us to know that the smallest thing shall not be forgotten.' She continues that, even when 'people suffer such terrible evils that it does not seem as though any good will ever come of them', then God comforts her with the thought that 'at the end of time you will truly see it in the fullness of joy'.

Anyone who lived as long as Julian did in the 14th century must have been familiar with pain: early death was commonplace and physical suffering something to be borne daily. How do we get away, though, from the uncomfortable feeling that this sense of everything being resolved in heaven is just 'pie in the sky when you die'—the dishonest get-out clause for all kinds of atrocities?

However much our faith can be travestied in this way by those who wish to destroy it, some of us still know that heaven is real. Some people's misguided thoughts about it don't make it any the less true. Dodgy versions of it just make it more important that we should alleviate suffering wherever we can—even if only in little ways, such as giving to charity, helping our neighbours and going the extra mile with those who are troubled.

REFLECTION
---

*Father, thank you for your reassurance that suffering and death
are not the end.*

After the vision—guided by God

Jesus saith unto her, Mary. She turned herself, and saith unto him,
Rabboni; which is to say, Master. Jesus saith unto her, Touch me not;
for I am not yet ascended to my Father: but go to my brethren, and
say unto them, I ascend unto my Father, and your Father; and to my
God, and your God.

Both Julian and Mary Magdalene had to move on from their meeting with
the divine and go back to their more ordinary lives, yet lives touched
by God. After the visions, Julian devoted her time to God's good use in her
offerings of prayer and spiritual counsel to her many visitors. She worked
out her vocation and pursued it wholeheartedly.

This could make her seem a long way from our humdrum offerings.
When set against those people who give their lives to God as nuns, missionaries, priests and other forms of full-time vocation, our ministry can
seem feeble.

This, though, is where Jesus' message to Mary Magdalene is so important: 'Don't cling to me… I have not yet ascended…'. To me, this suggests
that none of us can simply grab hold of God. He is not our possession.
When Jesus has ascended, the Father sends the Holy Spirit to guide us
on our various paths. We work out our salvation in fear and trembling
(Philippians 2:12).

For most of us, this means being in the quiet majority of faithful lay
Christians. We should not feel insignificant, as we are the powerhouse
of the Church. We are the people who represent our Lord in those many
different situations where, perhaps, 'professional' Christians don't end up
so often—in encounters with those who have little contact with church,
where we're not always expected to toe a religious line. Each day, the Holy
Spirit guides us to face all sorts of possibilities—what the Book of Common
Prayer calls 'all such good works as thou hast prepared for us to walk in'.

PRAYER

Christ has no body now on earth but yours. No hands but yours.
Yours are the feet with which he is to go about doing good.

Teresa of Avila

Knowing that you are loved

For I reckon that the sufferings of this present time are not worthy to be compared with the glory which shall be revealed in us. For the earnest expectation of the creature waiteth for the manifestation of the sons of God. For the creature was made subject to vanity, not willingly, but by reason of him who hath subjected the same in hope, Because the creature itself also shall be delivered from the bondage of corruption into the glorious liberty of the children of God.

This passage from Romans, which continues in the next reading, reflects several themes in Julian's writing. Julian conveys a strong sense of longing for heaven—not to escape from the pain of this world but, more positively, to be united with God, the love of her life. For Julian, this was part of her sense that only in heaven will humans see life in full. Then, it will no longer be 'through a glass, darkly' (as we saw in the readings from 1 Corinthians 13): we will have a true sense of what life is about and how suffering fits into the picture.

She writes of God's reassuring her that, in heaven, 'you shall have no kind of suffering, no kind of displeasure, no unfulfilled desire, but always joy and bliss'. In the chapter after that, she refers to the hints of heaven that we can have on earth: 'the people who in this life willingly choose God for love, may be sure they will be loved eternally, and it is this eternal love that works this grace in them'. God's presence now 'brings marvellous security' ('mervelous sekirness', or 'sureness' in medieval English), by 'sure hope through great love'.

This is surely what the world needs now, as we face insecurity, rapid change and the temporary nature of modern life. When it seems as if our dearest friends let us down, all our arrangements are built on shifting sands and we can't trust public figures, this is exactly what we need. The sure hope of God's eternal love is emphatically not an excuse for oppression by those with secular authority or even those with power in religious organisations, nor for bad faith and an attitude of 'I'll make it up to you later.' This strong love of God's is really the truth about our future, if only we would realise it.

PRAYER

Father, help me to see the universe, and my place in it,
from your eternal perspective.

All things work together for good

Likewise the Spirit also helpeth our infirmities: for we know not what we should pray for as we ought: but the Spirit itself maketh intercession for us with groanings which cannot be uttered. And he that searcheth the hearts knoweth what is the mind of the Spirit, because he maketh intercession for the saints according to the will of God. And we know that all things work together for good to them that love God, to them who are the called according to his purpose.

Following on from the previous passage about longing for God, Paul sets out how this can work. God knows us so intimately that he prays with us, deep within us, as part of the flow of love within the Trinity. This recalls parts of Julian's writing: 'our essential being is a creation within God ['our substance is a creture in God', in medieval English]; for the almighty truth of the Trinity is our father, he who made us and keeps us within him; and the deep wisdom of the Trinity is our mother, in whom we are all enclosed… in our essence we are in God, and God in us… for Christ works mercifully within us, and we are in accord with him by divine grace through the gifts and virtues of the Holy Spirit.'

This is surely the deepest comfort we can have in all our feeble attempts to be decent human beings: to know that God is with us in our striving—in our suffering and failure, as well as our mundane efforts at prayer. God is united with us: he is not some distant heavenly being.

The way Julian so movingly describes this is stirring, bearing as it does the marks of hard-won wisdom, arrived at after years of uncertainty and puzzling over the meaning of her visions. It's not the superficial, if hopeful, reassurance of 'I'm sure it'll be fine.' Instead, it's a rare gift of insight that can speak directly to our deepest fears about being out on our own and distant from God. Julian knows that God is within each one of us and can work through us. The end result is all things working together for good.

— REFLECTION —

'God hath sent forth the Spirit of his Son into your hearts, crying, "Abba, Father"' (Galatians 4:6).

Joined to God in love for ever

[Jesus said:] Again, the kingdom of heaven is like unto treasure hid in a field; the which when a man hath found, he hideth, and for joy thereof goeth and selleth all that he hath, and buyeth that field. Again, the kingdom of heaven is like unto a merchant man, seeking goodly pearls: Who, when he had found one pearl of great price, went and sold all that he had, and bought it.

After her visions, Julian became like the figures Jesus spoke of in these parables of the kingdom. She devoted her energies to prayer, giving spiritual counsel and writing, so that others might find God. This activity became the centre of her existence.

As we noted in the readings about Elijah, such extreme examples of God's gifts and human response can make Julian's experience seem a long way away from our little lives. They might inspire us, but perhaps in a way that fails to reach the heart of our unease. We may know that we can't give our lives to God in the same way that Julian did—many of us have husbands to feed, wives to care for or other responsibilities—but we can still do something. Are our lives really marked by prayer and the closeness to God that springs from it? Would anyone ever say that we were 'driven by God'? Why not?

We can all share in something like this cheerful enthusiasm for God. It doesn't mean we have to skip around and grin inanely. If we are centred in Christ, that fact will spill out in all sorts of ways, perhaps unshowy ones, yet definitely there.

This might be possible if we catch the vision from Julian of our lives with God being 'joined to him in love for ever'. That is, 'our life is all grounded and rooted in love, and without love we cannot live... our eternal support, our dwelling, our life and our being are all in God; for as his endless goodness protects us when we sin, so that we do not perish, the same endless goodness continually negotiates a peace in us, in place of our anger and our contentious falling.'

--- **PRAYER** ---

Father, draw me closer to you, in your great love.

The goodness that cannot be angry

[Jesus said:] O Jerusalem, Jerusalem, thou that killest the prophets, and stonest them which are sent unto thee, how often would I have gathered thy children together, even as a hen gathereth her chickens under her wings, and ye would not! Behold, your house is left unto you desolate. For I say unto you, Ye shall not see me henceforth, till ye shall say, Blessed is he that cometh in the name of the Lord.

One of Julian's most famous pieces of writing is her startling image of God as mother. It is sometimes misunderstood, especially by people who aren't familiar with the way that the Bible uses picture-language to describe what is essentially indefinable—God. What Julian did was to describe the Virgin Mary as the mother of us all and then write, 'And our Saviour is our true mother in whom we are eternally born, and by whom we shall always be enclosed.' You can tell she doesn't mean it literally.

Julian wasn't the first to reflect on the idea of God being like a mother. Other medieval writers used the image, such as St Anselm (who was Archbishop of Canterbury from 1093 to 1109). Julian, however, stands out, as she treats the idea more vividly. She outlines some of the characteristics of God's love for us, just as Jesus does in this Gospel passage. He is saying something about God's care, about how God wants to protect his children from harm.

Jesus' image is similar to Julian's, of being 'enclosed'. Both suggest comforting warmth and physical cherishing. Julian takes it further, though. She uses the image to work out the answer to one of the big questions of Christianity: how is it that a just God can deal with sinful humans? She reaches the conclusion that God can never be really angry because he loves us too much—like a father and mother: 'God is the goodness that cannot be angry, for he is nothing but goodness.' She can't figure this out rationally, so it becomes one of the things that God will resolve in heaven.

Thus, Julian's picture of God as mother, as well as father, isn't so much an early example of feminism but part of her deep sense of God's love. This is Julian all over—warm experience, developed, after much thought, into striking insight.

PRAYER

God, our father and mother, lead us into your truth today,
just as you led Julian.

The literary and historical value of the King James Version

Can a translation ever be as significant as an original? When thinking of the King James Bible and its impact on the literature, history and culture of English-speaking countries across the world, one is tempted to say 'yes'.

As we celebrate its quatercentenary, it is worth reflecting how much had changed in the 102 years between 1509, when Henry VIII (1491–1547) ascended to the English throne, and 1611, when his successor James VI and I (1566–1625) authorised the Bible that still bears his name.

MEDIEVAL BIBLICAL TRANSLATION

Although many individual parts of scripture were translated in medieval England, only one complete Bible translation was produced, by the religious radical John Wyclif (d. 1384) and other, unknown scholars in sympathy with his aims. Because they and their followers, the Lollards, were considered heretical, this Bible was largely suppressed and had little influence on what followed.

The medieval Church's awareness that the Bible was a difficult text tended to work against allowing unlearned people access to it, while the dominance of Latin within Western Christendom meant that St Jerome's Latin translation of the Bible, the Vulgate, had an international status that no Bible written in a living language could rival.

REFORMATION DEBATES

The new standards in literary scholarship set during the Renaissance, however, which were brought about by a widely shared urge to return to the earliest sources, created increasing dissatisfaction with the Vulgate. While many scholars sought advances in textual understanding as a means of increasing the Catholic Church's authority, the first Protestant leaders—Martin Luther (1483–1546), John Calvin (1509–1564) and others—believed that their research gave them no alternative but to break away from Catholicism. In part, this came about because the churches had different notions of what scripture was for and how best to deploy it.

The difference in weight given to scripture and tradition is one of the most important differences between Catholicism and Protestantism at this date: Catholics saw the faith as being handed down through the centuries by a combination of scripture and church tradition, while Protestant thinkers tended to suspect tradition, placing more emphasis on scripture and the practices of the early Church as recorded in the New Testament.

All important Protestant thinkers believed that detailed personal engagement with the Bible was essential for the Christian, which galvanised both translators and readers. Although English Christians suffered many losses to their worship during the country's long metamorphosis into a Protestant nation, the growing place of Bible reading within ordinary Christian life compensated for much.

THE BEGINNINGS OF PRINT

The Reformation era was the first to benefit from the widespread circulation of Bibles translated into modern languages. Religious and technological innovation were closely interrelated here. In medieval times, when texts could be circulated only by being read out loud or copied by hand, the practicalities of supplying scripture to a wide audience were tricky to surmount. But the advent of printing changed matters, making it possible to distribute authoritative copies of scripture with unprecedented cheapness and ease.

This had many effects. Since direct access to the Bible was no longer the preserve of the educated or wealthy, it followed that those who could read their native tongue, but not Latin, were an important, relatively untapped market. Within theology, this new availability of scripture was to revolutionise notions of what Christians should know in order to be saved. The Protestant emphasis on reading and interpreting the Bible for yourself would have been impossible without print, and helped to inspire literacy. Many people, especially women and those from the lower orders, now wanted to learn to read specifically in order to read the Bible.

BIBLE TRANSLATION IN REFORMATION ENGLAND

Compared to many countries on the Continent, Catholic as well as Protestant, England's religious leaders were backward in taking advantage of the new technology. This was partly because the earlier association of scripture translation with Lollardry (which was still seen as heretical) had not helped its cause within the religious mainstream.

Despite the break with Rome that took place during his reign, Henry VIII was innately conservative on religious issues, and saw the era's first attempt at an English Bible as enough of a threat for him to put the translator, William Tyndale (c. 1494–1536), to death. Later in his reign, though, as head of a Church that had taken on several Protestant features, Henry was to do a U-turn. The material that Tyndale had left—all the New Testament, and much of the Old—served as the basis for two complete translations, one by Miles Coverdale (1488–1569) and the other by 'Thomas Matthew', the pseudonym of John Rogers (c. 1500–55).

The work of both was licensed and, together with 'Taverner's Bible', a revision of Thomas Matthew's work, served as the basis for the so-called 'Great Bible', the first to be made available in churches. Thus, despite his martyr's end, Tyndale—perhaps the most distinctive prose stylist in the history of the English Bible—had a profound influence on later, mainstream translators.

A wide choice of different translations and revisions were published in the reign of Edward VI (1537–53) under a Protestant regime less concerned than Henry's about uniformity, but under Elizabeth I (1533–1603) the 'Great Bible' was revised and retitled 'The Bishops' Bible'.

In between these monarchs, public use of the Bible was banned during England's five-year return to Catholicism under Mary I (1516–58), a circumstance which, ironically, gave rise to another translation, the Geneva Bible. Originally the product of English Protestant religious exiles on the Continent, this came to be the most widely read Bible translation in Elizabethan and early Jacobean England, despite the fact that it was never endorsed by the English Church. It appears to have been the favourite Bible of William Shakespeare (1564–1616), which tells us less about his religious sympathies than about the fact that it was the most user-friendly of the English Bibles on offer to his generation. It was affordably priced and a comfortable size to carry about, with extensive, if sometimes controversial, marginal notes.

The ever-increasing association of biblical translation with Protestantism had made the Catholic Church warier of it than in earlier days, yet the need to cater for Elizabethan England's beleaguered Catholic population did inspire the exiled priest Gregory Martin (?1542–82) to inaugurate a translation for them, the Douai Bible.

THE MAKING OF THE KING JAMES BIBLE

The translators involved on all these projects were inspired by the most up-to-date scholarly standards of the age, which involved checking several manuscripts against each other and trying to establish which readings were the earliest and most authoritative.

Thus there was a massive body of previous expertise to draw on when the team responsible for the King James Bible began their work. Even so, theirs was an impressive achievement: the project was accomplished in a very short time (eight years) and with immense managerial effectiveness. Forty-seven scholars were involved in translating, and each translator's work had to be scrutinised by a group, while two individuals from each of the three centres of translation—Westminster, Oxford and Cambridge—were responsible for overseeing the complete text and preparing it for publication. A careful balance was struck between unity and diversity (each team member was neither to go out on a limb from the others nor to impose a misleading uniformity) and experts in various languages were consulted.

Being able to draw on so many different types of expertise lent the project huge intellectual authority, at a time when the Church of England, beset by Catholics on one side and Puritan separatists on the other, especially needed to show its strength. But the epithet 'Authorised Version', by which the King James Bible is also known, refers to the royal backing that was just as crucial to its status.

One of James VI and I's first acts, when he succeeded to the combined thrones of England and Scotland in 1603, had been to call a meeting with his bishops to discuss the possibility of a new translation that reflected his hierarchical notions of Church and state. At a politically sensitive time, the Geneva Bible's downplaying of a king's role and government by bishops demanded robust counteraction.

Other reasons, too, make it appropriate that James should be permanently associated with this version of scripture. As perhaps the most theologically literate monarch that England has ever had, he saw his headship of the Church of England as an opportunity to educate his people and bring about greater understanding between the religious factions of his time.

This ecumenical aim could only have been helped by the translators' debt to the Protestant pioneers of an earlier generation. This is a debt that comes over in thousands of echoes, making the experience of reading the King James Bible one of hearing many voices.

The team was operating at a fortunate historical moment, benefiting from previous translators' good ideas but able to refine them. But this respect for past scholars also had an effect on the style of the King James Bible, at a time when the English language was changing at enormous speed. Much of its vocabulary and syntax would have come across as old-fashioned, even to its first audiences, and 400 years later many passages now need translation themselves.

Yet this unfamiliarity has also enhanced the aesthetic experience that the King James Bible offers, instilling a sense of awe in its hearers and helping to define what we think of as high style. Remarkably, for most of its history, its elevated language has not limited its accessibility. From the time of its publication, it has had a profound effect on the English language and the national imagination at all social levels, from the educated to those who were unable to read it but heard it read out loud.

THE KING JAMES BIBLE AND POPULAR CULTURE

Designed from the first to be heard as well as perused, the King James Bible became more widely familiar than any other text, through being read aloud in church and within household worship. For generations of Englishmen who had received only an elementary education, learning and Christianity went hand in hand. As the best prose model they were likely to encounter, it taught them both a faith and a literary style.

The Pilgrim's Progress, written by the self-taught John Bunyan, remains one of English literature's most sustained attempts to imitate biblical narrative, while its more introspective moments remind us of the powerful influence biblical poetry has had on Christian self-examination. When the hero Christian meets a man in an iron cage and asks how he came to be in this condition, the man's reply is patterned like a psalm: 'I left off to watch, and be sober; I laid the reins upon the neck of my lusts; I sinned against the light of the word, and the goodness of God; I have grieved the Spirit, and he is gone…'

For the illiterate and barely literate, the King James Bible provided a storehouse of metaphor and proverbial wisdom, as shown by the rustic characters in the novels of Thomas Hardy (1840–1928). Concerned that the rural culture he knew as a boy was dying off, Hardy had a historian's interest in recording peasants' language and thought patterns, while deploying them as only a sophisticated creative writer could.

In the final passage of *Far from the Madding Crowd*, for instance, Joseph Poorgrass's comment on the wedding of Gabriel Oak to the *femme fatale* Bathsheba Everdene strikes a note of foreboding: 'I wish him joy o' her; though I were once or twice upon saying today with holy Hosea, in my scripture manner, "Ephraim is joined to idols: let him alone"' (Hosea 4:17).

'THE BIBLE AS LITERATURE'

From its first appearance, the King James Bible would also have informed the work and worship of those who benefited from a university education. But the study of the Bible from a purely literary point of view came later in the day, as English literature and the English language made their way into the university curriculum in the 19th century.

The literary importance of the King James Bible gave it a claim to be studied alongside classical literature as a source and inspiration for literature written in the English tongue; but, for many from the mid-Victorian era to the present day, Judaism and Christianity deserved no more respect than the religions of ancient Greece and Rome.

It is significant that Percy Bysshe Shelley (1792–1822), notorious in the early 19th century as a scoffer at established religion, was one of the first to distinguish literary and devotional modes of reading the Bible. His fellow poet Lord Byron (1788–1824) described him as a 'great admirer of scripture as a composition', a suggestive anticipation of the phrase familiar to us now, 'the Bible as literature'. In the present day, as secularism and religious diversity have led to unfamiliarity with the Bible, teaching it as an aid to understanding Britain's literary heritage has become more essential than ever.

As if to bear out the prediction of the Victorian commentator Matthew Arnold (1822–88) that literature would come to fulfil some of the needs previously met by religion, the growth of agnosticism and atheism as respectable intellectual options has, if anything, confirmed the literary eminence of the King James Version.

Translators of religious texts have often recognised the difficulties inherent in reconciling truth and literary elegance—a tension that can be seen in English writers from the Wycliffites onwards—and it has proved possible for many latter-day readers to discount the truth claims of the King James Bible while continuing to enjoy its narrative drive, quotability and evocations of transcendence.

The notion that several books of the Old Testament are best read as legendary—scandalous to the Victorians, standard to most today—has contributed to this development, as has the view that human creativity can be seen as a way of working alongside God rather than in opposition to him. Most Christians now would see nothing wrong with the idea of acknowledging the Bible's literary merit and power to inspire imaginative writers.

Even so, creative responses to the King James Bible have led in some highly original directions, even in earlier centuries, and even among those who would not have questioned that the Bible was the word of God.

LITERARY REREADINGS OF THE KING JAMES BIBLE

One literary rereading was John Milton's (1608–74), whose *Paradise Lost* is well-known for its subversive depiction of Satan as more engaging than God. Intermingling the books of Genesis and Revelation, Milton's poem evokes many other places in the Bible, too.

Eve, resisting the serpent in Book 9, explains how God has forbidden her and Adam to eat from the tree of knowledge: 'God so commanded, and left that command / Sole daughter of his voice; the rest, we live / Law to ourselves, our reason is our law' (652–4). Picking up the allusion to St Paul's description of the Gentiles as 'a law unto themselves' (Romans 2:14) helps us realise what Milton is doing here. As he implies, Eve's obedience to God's commands is only skin-deep, and, like the Gentiles, she is all too ready to live by her own law rather than his. In this retelling of an Old Testament story, Milton's glance forward to the New Testament prepares us for the story of the Fall.

The more secular notion of paradise evoked by W.B. Yeats (1865–1939) illustrates how the language of the King James Bible can be transferred out of religious contexts altogether, while still carrying a spiritual charge. One of his best-known lines, 'I will arise and go now, and go to Innisfree', derives from the words of the repentant prodigal son: 'I will arise and go to my father' (Luke 15:18). The allusion, surprising at first, makes sense if one sees it as heralding another kind of conversion—away from the city and towards the purity of nature, re-establishing contact not with one's divine father but with mother earth.

William Blake (1757–1827), the purveyor of a semi-Christian but highly biblical religion, achieves something analogous in his poem 'Jerusalem', when he dissociates himself from the 'dark satanic mills' of industrial England to anticipate the day when the holy city will arise from her 'green and pleasant land'. Blake's readership would have been as steeped in the King James Bible as he was himself, and they would have recognised the tradition within which he was speaking when he commandeered imagery from the prophetic visions of the Old Testament: 'Bring me my spear. O clouds, unfold! / Bring me my chariot of fire!'

THE KING JAMES BIBLE AND HYMN WRITERS

'Lo, He comes with clouds descending', the well-known Advent hymn written by Charles Wesley (1707–88), exploits a similar prophetic strain for more mainstream purposes, reminding us how influential the King James Bible has been for hymn writers, Anglican as well as Methodist and others from the Free Churches. Although this particular hymn is very closely inspired by the book of Revelation—'Behold, he cometh with clouds; and every eye shall see him, and they also which pierced him: and all kindreds of the earth shall wail because of him' (Revelation 2:7)—the book of Psalms has been the most significant influence of all on hymn writers in English.

Here, the King James Bible has coexisted with other English translations, especially the metrical psalms which, from the 16th century to the 19th, were commonly bound together with the Book of Common Prayer and used in church worship.

Both kinds of versification fed into the work of religious poets. Rhyming psalms were perhaps the most important model for hymn writers, and for religious poets as different as George Herbert (1593–1633) and William Cowper (1731–1800), but the psalms of the King James Bible, written in rhythmical parallelistic prose echoing the Hebrew originals, came into their own when they inspired the pioneers of free verse.

In *Leaves of Grass*, the American poet Walt Whitman (1819–92) used psalmic repetition to echo the words of Genesis's creator-God: 'Whither I walk I cannot define, but I know that it is good, / The whole universe indicates that it is good, / The past and the present indicate that it is good.'

THE KING JAMES BIBLE IN AMERICA

With its tales of slavery and liberation, and its influence on the rhetoric of preachers and political campaigners, the King James Bible has also profoundly affected the subject matter and style of African-American writing. In recent years, perhaps its most striking appearance has been in the novel *Beloved* by the black American writer Toni Morrison (b. 1931), a harrowing story of child murder and haunting that comments on the life of American slaves through evoking the Song of Songs: 'I am black, but comely' (1:5); 'love is strong as death; jealousy is cruel as the grave' (8:6).

In other respects, too, the King James Bible has had a prominent part to play in the diverse religious cultures of the United States. It remains the translation preferred in many circumstances by the Gideon Bible movement, a body founded in the United States which distributes Bibles to hotel rooms, and it heavily influenced the Book of Mormon, a testament held to be sacred by the Church of Jesus Christ of Latter-Day Saints.

While the Church of England can be proud of bringing the King James Bible into the world, it is no one Church's exclusive property. The past endeavour of missionaries across the world means that it has influenced every country where the English language is spoken and the Christian faith adhered to.

THE LEGACY OF THE KING JAMES BIBLE

Within England, the older generation will remember the King James Bible being read in church on a regular basis. But the past 150 years have also brought to birth many alternative versions of the scriptures—the Revised Standard Version, the New International Version, the Good News Bible, the Jerusalem Bible and others. Given this competition, what has the King James Bible to offer us today? Many of its translations, after all, have been superseded, and, as with approaches to worship, the days of Anglican uniformity are over for good.

Like another touchstone of traditional Anglicanism, the Book of Common Prayer, it has not been forgotten. It retains an honoured place in Anglican worship, especially on occasions and in venues where thanksgiving for the Church's historical legacy and cultural richness is particularly appropriate, and within the traditions of many other Christian bodies.

Through its own remarkable prose and poetry, and its influence on Britain's literature and oral culture, it has touched the lives of secular audiences and those of different religions. To Christian believers, it hints at a God who incarnates beauty in the prose, poetry and scholarship of a particular historical moment.

Dr Alison Shell teaches in the English Department of University College, London. She was formerly Professor of English Literature at Durham University. She is the author of *Oral Culture and Catholicism in Early Modern England* (Cambridge University Press, 2007) and *Catholicism, Controversy and the English Literary Imagination, 1558–1660* (Cambridge University Press, 1999).

About
brf:

BRF is a registered charity and also a limited company, and has been in existence since 1922. Through all that we do—producing resources, providing training, working face-to-face with adults and children, and via the web—we work to resource individuals and church communities in their Christian discipleship through the Bible, prayer and worship.

Our Barnabas children's team works with primary schools and churches to help children under 11, and the adults who work with them, to explore Christianity creatively and to bring the Bible alive.

To find out more about BRF and its core activities and ministries, visit:

www.brf.org.uk
www.brfonline.org.uk
www.barnabasinschools.org.uk
www.barnabasinchurches.org.uk
www.messychurch.org.uk
www.foundations21.org.uk

If you have any questions about BRF and our work, please email us at

enquiries@brf.org.uk